CONTEMPORARY EARTRAINING

LEVEL TWO

BY MARK HARRISON

ISBN 0-8256-9393-4

HARRISON
MUSIC
EDUCATION
SYSTEMS

HAL•LEONARD®
CORPORATION

7777 W. BLUEMOUND RD. P.O. BOX 13819 MILWAUKEE, WI 53213

Copyright © 1994 by HAL LEONARD CORPORATION
International Copyright Secured   All Rights Reserved

No part of this publication may be reproduced in any form or by any means
without the prior written permission of the Publisher.

Visit Hal Leonard Online at
www.halleonard.com

Welcome to *Contemporary Eartraining Level 2*. This book has been used by **hundreds of students** in Eartraining classes held at the former **Grove School of Music**, and is now used in many schools worldwide including our own **Harrison School of Music** in Los Angeles. As such this book represents a proven and 'battle-tested' approach to the subject matter! For many years the internationally-acclaimed Grove School provided a unique learning experience for the contemporary musician, and in this exciting environment I developed a complete Eartraining syllabus which became a vital part of the school's musicianship instruction. I am delighted that my Eartraining Level 1 & 2 courses are now available to a worldwide market of students and educators! This book is self-sufficient for teachers working in private lesson or classroom situations, and for students wishing to use it as a theory/conceptual review. However, teachers as well as students working on a self-study basis will be interested to know that **cassette tapes of all the exercises in this book are available** - please see page *vi* for further information.

Some of you may be thinking, "What is Eartraining and why do I need it?" - well, it's my belief that an educated ear is the foundation we need in order to compose, arrange or perform in contemporary styles. In other words - you won't be able to write or play anything that you can't hear! A main factor distinguishing top pro musicians from the rest, is their ability to 'hear ahead' - to know what something will sound like **before** it is written or played. This of course results in greater focus and accuracy in the musical end product. Also the ability to hear what other performers are doing, either live or transcribing from records, is a vital goal for a great many musicians! The bottom line is that **the mastery of Eartraining skills will enable you to achieve these goals!**

My Eartraining books & courses use a key-center based 'relative pitch' method. By this I mean that the ear first needs to identify where the tonic or 'home-base' of a given key is, and then to establish the 'active-to-resting' resolutions that occur within the key. There are two vital consequences to this approach - firstly it empowers you to discard bad habits like 'singing up the scale' to find out where you are, and secondly you will be identifying the 'resolutions' in every key in exactly the same manner. In order to do this, we need a method of labelling the scale degrees which will apply to all keys - my books use the '**SOLFEG**' (short for 'solfeggio') system. This simply entails calling the major scale degrees by their 'solfeg' names - **DO, RE, MI, FA, SO, LA, TI** and back to **DO**. Famous 'solfeg' users include Julie Andrews in the Sound of Music!! The beauty of using this system is that '**DO**' can be assigned to **any key** - the scale resolutions will work in exactly the same manner! Indeed I believe that it is vital for the modern musician to be able to hear melody and harmony in the same way regardless of the actual key used - hence the problems with the so-called eartraining methods advocating 'perfect pitch' that I sometimes see advertised. My *Contemporary Eartraining Level 1* book introduced this '**SOLFEG**' labelling system and the main 'active-to-resting' resolutions which occur within the major scale - these tools were then used in melodic dictation, diatonic chord recognition etc. This *Contemporary Eartraining Level 2* book also makes use of these '**SOLFEG**' and resolution concepts - please check out the 'Level 1 Solfeg Review' on page 2 as necessary!

AUTHOR'S FOREWORD

Here in *Contemporary Eartraining Level 2* our main focus is on hearing harmony and different types of chord progressions (following on from *Contemporary Eartraining Level 1* where the main focus was on hearing melodies, resolutions and intervals). In this book we will be transcribing chord progressions using major triads (involving key changes) and diatonic triads (staying within the same key). These types of progressions are routinely found in today's pop music! Also we will be transcribing 'II-V-I'-type four-part chord progressions (for example, **Dmi7 - G7 - Cma7** in the key of C) moving through different key changes - this is an essential foundation for understanding jazz and standard tunes. We then see how melodies can be used (and transcribed) across these 'II-V-I'-type modulations. As so much of today's music uses modal scales, we will also work on modal scale recognition in this book. To get the best out of the material in *Level 2*, you need to have some familiarity with basic melodic dictation and interval recognition, either by having worked through my *Contemporary Eartraining Level 1* course, or via equivalent study and/or experience.

This book is divided into three main sections:-
- **Textbook**, containing chapters for each subject area addressed, with explanation of the eartraining concepts and how to apply them
- **Workbook Questions**, containing exercises for each subject area
- **Workbook Answers**, containing answers and transcribed voicings for all the exercises.

At the **Harrison School of Music**, we typically cover this material in a ten-week class 'quarter', although the material can of course be adapted for use within different course lengths (i.e. a different number of weeks), at the discretion of the teacher or educational institution. The cassette tapes available with the book contain practice material and homework assignments for each chapter.

Note to teachers - when using this book in private or group class situations, you can play from the 'Workbook Answers' section when drilling your students - they can then fill out their answers in the corresponding 'Workbook Questions' section. For students wishing to drill the material on a self-study basis, you can listen to the cassette tapes which are available (see page *vi*) when filling out the Workbook Questions - this can be verified against the Workbook Answers. Also, teachers using this material may feel that it is productive for the students to be using the tapes between classes - this is certainly true in my own experience!

Good luck with Eartraining - and I hope it opens many doors for you as a musician!

Mark Harrison

Harrison Music Education Systems

Los Angeles, California

MARK HARRISON is a keyboardist, composer and educator with over twenty years experience in the industry. Before moving to Los Angeles in 1987, Mark's musical career in his native London included appearances on British national (**BBC**) television as well as extensive club and studio experience. As an active composer for television in both England and the United States, his work is heard internationally in commercials for clients like **American Express** and **CNN**, as well as in **A & E**'s popular **American Justice** series.

Mark was commissioned by the music equipment manufacturers **Roland** and **Gibson** to compose and arrange music for their trade shows, and in 1996 Boston's renowned **Berklee College of Music** invited Mark to showcase his composition **First Light** with Berklee's faculty orchestra. Active in the Los Angeles music scene, Mark has also performed with top professional musicians including **Bruce Hornsby**'s drummer John Molo; **Yanni**'s bassist Rick Fierabracci; and **Ray Charles**' bassist Adam Cohen.

After teaching at the internationally-acclaimed **Grove School of Music** for six years, Mark founded the **Harrison School of Music** (a successor institution to the Grove school) in Los Angeles. His groundbreaking keyboard method **The Pop Piano Book** is endorsed by Grammy-winners **Russell Ferrante** and **Mark James**, as well as other top professional musicians and educators. **Keyboard Magazine** calls Mark's presentation style "warm, humorous and clear", and names The Pop Piano Book "the most accessible and valuable keyboard method available for those interested in popular styles".

Mark has authored numerous music instruction books (including comprehensive methods for music theory and eartraining), and the **Harrison Music Education Systems** product line is published internationally by **Hal Leonard Publications**. Mark's methods are also used at many educational institutions (including the internationally-famous **Berklee College of Music**) and his books & tapes have been purchased by thousands of students in over twenty-five countries worldwide. Mark continues to be in demand as a uniquely effective contemporary music educator, both in the classroom and in his private teaching studio in Los Angeles.

CASSETTE TAPES are available with this book!

The *CONTEMPORARY EARTRAINING LEVEL TWO BOOK* contains hundreds of music drills and exercises.

If you are a **student** who would like to work through this material on a self-study basis, or if you are a **teacher** who feels that this self-study option would be of value to your students, you'll be interested to know that all these exercises are available *RECORDED ON TAPE* - a total of over three hours of material on three cassette tapes. If you would like to order or inquire about these tapes, please call toll-free (in the U.S.):

(4 6 3 7)
1-800-799-HMES

(**H**arrison **M**usic **E**ducation **S**ystems)

or check out our website at:

www.harrisonmusic.com

or you may write to us at:

HARRISON MUSIC EDUCATION SYSTEMS
P.O. BOX 56505
SHERMAN OAKS
CA 91413 USA

'Contemporary Eartraining Level 2' ©1994 Mark Harrison. All Rights Reserved.
'Contemporary Eartraining Level 2' Second Edition ©1998 Mark Harrison. All Rights Reserved.

Here are some other books available from

HARRISON MUSIC EDUCATION SYSTEMS:-

Contemporary Eartraining Level One

A modern eartraining approach to help you hear and transcribe melodies, rhythms, intervals, bass lines and basic chords (available with four cassette tapes of vocal drills and exercises). Developed at the **Grove School of Music** in Los Angeles.

The Pop Piano Book

A complete method for playing contemporary styles spontaneously on the keyboard. This **500-page** book includes application of harmony to the keyboard in all keys, and then specific instruction for playing in pop, rock, funk, country, ballad, new age and gospel styles. Endorsed by **Grammy**-winners and **Keyboard Magazine**, this book is available with cassette tapes and MIDI files of all 800 music examples!

Contemporary Music Theory Level One

This introductory pop & jazz theory course covers music notation, major and minor scales, key signatures, intervals, triads, four-part chords, modes, diatonic chords, suspensions, and alterations of 3- and 4-part chords. Includes hundreds of written theory exercises, all with answers provided!

Contemporary Music Theory Level Two

This intermediate pop & jazz theory course covers 'II-V-I' progressions in major and minor keys, five-part chords, substitutions, harmonic analysis of pop & jazz tunes, voiceleading, use of 'upper structure' voicings, and pentatonic & blues scale applications. Includes hundreds of written theory exercises with answers!

...and we're working on the following book to be released soon:

Contemporary Music Theory Level Three

This more advanced pop & jazz theory course covers chord extensions, alterations and scale sources for **all** major, minor, dominant and diminished chords, and then how to apply this to your composing/arranging/playing using our **contemporary shape concept**. Includes hundreds of written theory exercises with answers!

Your product inquiries are welcome - please see previous page for contact information!

- *The HARRISON SCHOOL OF MUSIC (based in Los Angeles, CA) is running group Eartraining classes using our Eartraining books!*

- *The school also offers Keyboard and Music Theory classes based on the acclaimed methods from HARRISON MUSIC EDUCATION SYSTEMS (see page vii), as well as guitar, bass, vocal, rhythm, songwriting, arranging, improvisation and ensemble classes.*

- *School founder MARK HARRISON was on the faculty at the internationally-acclaimed GROVE SCHOOL OF MUSIC for several years. The success of the Grove School proved that there was a need for high quality pop & jazz education taught by working professionals - this is now being provided in the Los Angeles area by the HARRISON SCHOOL OF MUSIC!*

If you would like to inquire about the school, or about private instruction with Mark Harrison, please call toll-free (in the U.S.):

(6 8 7 4)
1-800-828-MUSIC

or check out our website at:

www.harrisonmusic.com

or you may write to us at:

HARRISON SCHOOL OF MUSIC
P.O. BOX 56505
SHERMAN OAKS
CA 91413 USA

DICK GROVE

During the period from 1988 until 1992 I had the pleasure and privilege of teaching a wide range of courses at the **Grove School of Music**, in Los Angeles, California. From the time that **Dick Grove** founded this school in 1973 until the school's closure in 1992, his unique perspective on contemporary music influenced literally thousands of musicians and students from all around the world, as well as those of us on the faculty who were fortunate enough to work in this exceptional institution.

My experience on the Grove School faculty provided an ideal environment for me to develop and fine-tune my own concepts of how contemporary music should be taught, which in turn has helped me create my own series of instruction books and methods. Dick Grove's overall philosophy and concepts of contemporary music were very influential in this process, and I am proud to have been an integral part of the Grove School educational environment.

We were very saddened to hear of Dick's untimely death in December of 1998. I had the honor of speaking at a memorial service held for Dick in Los Angeles, which was attended by several hundred members of the 'Grove community'. Dick was a major influence and inspiration for the **Harrison School of Music**, and we know his legacy and spirit will continue to impact the many lives he has touched.

Mark Harrison

x

Contemporary Eartraining Level 2 by Mark Harrison

In **Contemporary Eartraining Level 1** we used 'solfeg' syllables to describe the major scale degrees, as follows:-

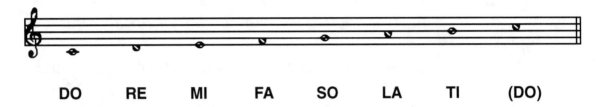

DO   RE   MI   FA   SO   LA   TI   (DO)

As I mentioned in the foreword, an important advantage of using solfeg is the ability to re-assign **DO** to any key. Our goal is to hear scale degree movements and resolutions the same way regardless of the key being used. The above syllables are sometimes referred to as 'diatonic' solfeg, as they are contained within the major scale (in this case C major).

If **DO** has been established as the key center or 'tonic', the remaining diatonic scale degrees will exhibit 'active or resting' properties, as follows:-

(DO), MI, SO	- These are the resting tones. They represent points of resolution or completion in melodies and harmonies.
FA, TI	- These are the 'active half-steps', so-called because they are a half-step step away from adjacent resting tones. Due to the strong 'leading' quality of the half-step, the resulting resolutions **FA to MI** and **TI to DO** are the strongest in any major key.
RE, LA	- These are the 'active whole-steps', so-called because they are a whole-step away from adjacent resting tones. The resulting resolutions **RE to DO** (or **MI**) and **LA to SO** are not as strong as the above half-step movements, due to the less 'leading' quality of the whole-step interval.

Hearing these resolutions (in any key) formed the cornerstone of our approach to transcribing melodies and intervals in **Contemporary Eartraining Level 1**. Now in this book we will expand on the solfeg concept by adding 'chromatic' solfeg syllables for those tones which do not belong in the major scale of the key being used, and by discussing the concepts of **Fixed 'DO'** and **Moveable 'DO'**. These concepts are addressed in Chapter 3 (page 11).

1.   *Introduction*

1.1.   This course functions as a second-level Eartraining method and builds on the foundation established in **Contemporary Eartraining Level 1**. First we will be developing our understanding of the 'circle-of-fifths' and 'circle-of-fourths' as a vehicle to enable us to hear key changes moving around the circle. *(SEE CHAPTER TWO)*

1.2.   We will also extend the '**SOLFEG**' concepts first introduced in Level 1, to include tones which are chromatic to (i.e. do not belong in) the major scale of the key signature being used, and we will develop the ideas of **Fixed 'DO'** and **Moveable 'DO'** as two alternate ways of approaching a piece of music. *(SEE CHAPTER THREE)*

1.3.   The first application of the 'circle-of-fifths' and 'circle-of-fourths' will be to hear major triad progressions moving between adjacent keys on the circle, followed by progressions using half-step movements. *(SEE CHAPTER FOUR)*

1.4.   We will work on recognizing the diatonic triad progressions which are widely used in contemporary music styles. In order to do this we must develop 'vertical' skills (hearing chord quality) and 'horizontal' skills (hearing voiceleading, commontones, and root intervals). The 'active' and/or 'resting' qualities of the diatonic triads will also be critical factors. *(SEE CHAPTER FIVE)*

1.5.   Modal scale recognition will also be studied. A significant percentage of contemporary music uses modal scale sources. Also the various 'momentary' key changes that are typically used on jazz and standard tunes, can be thought of as modal alterations to the 'home base' key - so hearing modal scales in this way can be a significant short-cut to recognizing key changes. *(SEE CHAPTER SIX)*

1.6.   A further application of the 'circle-of-fifths' and 'circle-of-fourths' will be as a framework within which to hear four-part 'II-V-I' progressions (i.e. **Dmi7 - G7 - Cma7** in the key of **C**) moving between different keys. This type of modulation is routinely used in jazz and standard tunes. *(SEE CHAPTER SEVEN)*

1.7.   The four-part 'II-V-I' progressions mentioned above, can of course be used to harmonize melodies (as in many standard tunes for example). We will work on transcribing melodies using the definitive **3rds** and **7ths** of these chords (referred to as the **7-3 lines**) moving across these key changes. *(SEE CHAPTER EIGHT)*

1.8.   Vocal drills are also included, as a practice vehicle to hear the various concepts moving around the 'circle-of-fifths' and 'circle-of-fourths'. *(SEE CHAPTER NINE)*

1.9.   Workbook questions and correct answers on all the above areas are also provided.

Explanation of 'circle-of-fifths' and 'circle-of-fourths'

2.1. The terms 'circle-of-fifths' and 'circle-of-fourths' are unfortunately subject to widely differing interpretations, not only by music students but also by professionals and educators! The way in which these concepts are defined in this chapter, may be new to you - but don't worry if you initially learnt the 'circles' in a different way - it's really only terminology! I hope to persuade you that this interpretation is not only more 'foolproof' but more accurately reflects *how the ear works* as we hear progressions moving around the circle. Effectively the terms 'circle-of-fifths' and 'circle-of-fourths' both refer to the same circle viewed in different ways i.e. moving in opposite directions.

2.2. First we will review the 'tetrachord' concept as a building block for major scales. In this context a tetrachord simply means a four-note group which is part of a larger scale relationship, as in the following example of a C major scale:-

(**WS** = whole-step, and **HS** = half-step)

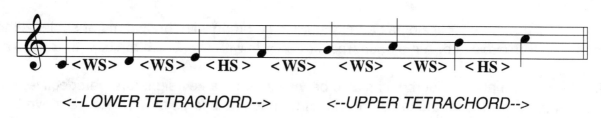

<--LOWER TETRACHORD-->   <--UPPER TETRACHORD-->

2.3. For our purposes here the important aspect to notice is that the lower and upper tetrachord of a major scale have the same interval construction i.e. wholestep-wholestep-halfstep. It therefore follows that each tetrachord with this construction will be present in two different major scales. In this case the lower tetrachord of the C major scale (C-D-E-F) is also the upper tetrachord of an F major scale, and the upper tetrachord of the C major scale (G-A-B-C) is also the lower tetrachord of a G major scale. We could then take these major scales (F and G) and see which other major scales they had tetrachords in common with, and so forth. If we continued this process through all keys we would arrive at the following series of relationships (see following page):-

(2.3. contd)

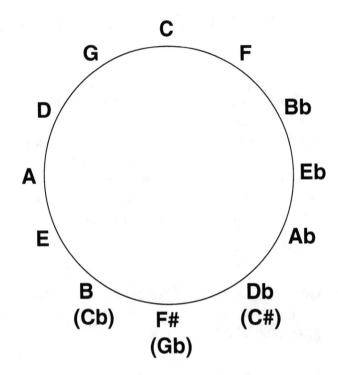

       Each major scale has a tetrachord in common with the two major scales either side of it on the 'circle', i.e. **A** major shares tetrachords with **D** & **E**, **Eb** major with **Bb** & **Ab** etc.

2.4.   The above diagram can also be viewed from a key-signature perspective. We know that the key of **C** (at the top of the circle) requires no sharps or flats. As we move to the right on the circle, we see that the key of **F** requires one flat, the key of **Bb** requires two flats, and so on. Conversely, as we move to the left, we see that the key of **G** requires one sharp, the key of **D** requires two sharps, etc. Each successive scale requires one further alteration to the key signature than the previous scale. For these reasons the right-hand part of the circle is often referred to as the 'flat' side, whereas the left-hand part of the circle is often referred to as the 'sharp' side.

2.5.   We can now see why this circle is referred to as the 'circle-of-fifths' or 'circle-of-fourths'. Each interval between consecutive notes on the circle is either a fourth or a fifth depending on whether the interval is considered to be ascending or descending. However because the intervals can be interpreted in these different ways, we need a more foolproof method for defining the difference between 'circle-of-fifths' or 'circle-of-fourths'.

2.6.   To do this we will consider the harmonic aspects of the circle. If each stage on the circle represented a major triad for example, what are the implications when we move between adjacent chords on the circle? Let us consider the following situation:-

FOR FURTHER INFORMATION ON DERIVING THE CIRCLE-OF-5THS & CIRCLE-OF-4THS, PLEASE REFER TO CHAPTER 1 OF OUR CONTEMPORARY MUSIC THEORY LEVEL 1 BOOK (SEE PAGE VII IN THIS BOOK).

2.6. contd.

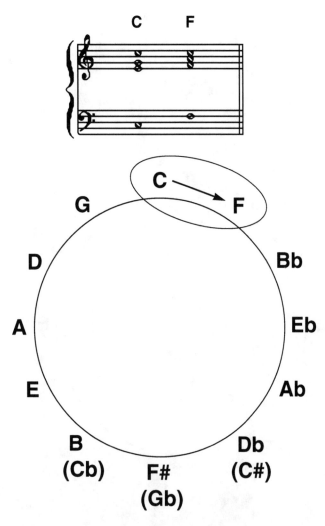

In this case we are moving from a **C** major triad to an **F** major triad. Let us further assume that the second chord represents the tonic of a new key i.e. in this case we are in the key of **F**. Therefore this movement represents a **V-to-I** (five-to-one) progression in the key of **F**. In a similar fashion, each successive pair of chords going clockwise on the circle represents a **V-to-I** relationship i.e.

- **F** to **Bb**   is a **V-to-I** in the key of **Bb**
- **Bb** to **Eb**   is a **V-to-I** in the key of **Eb**
- **Eb** to **Ab**   is a **V-to-I** in the key of **Ab**

and so forth.

2.7.   Now let us consider a counter-clockwise situation as follows (see over page):-

2.7. contd.

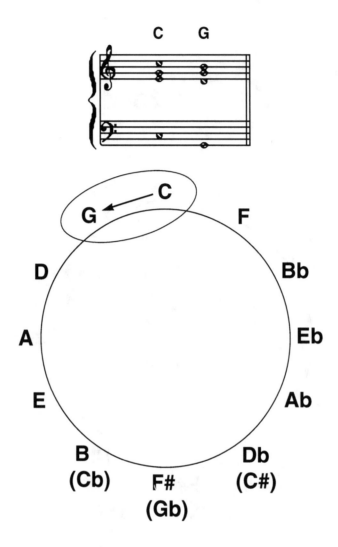

In this case we are moving from a **C** major triad to a **G** major triad. Again we will assume that the second chord represents the tonic of a new key i.e. in this case we are in the key of **G**. Therefore this movement represents a **IV-to-I** (four-to-one) progression in the key of **G**. In a similar fashion, each successive pair of chords going counter-clockwise on the circle represents a **IV-to-I** relationship i.e.

-     **G** to **D**   is a **IV-to-I** in the key of **D**
-     **D** to **A**   is a **IV-to-I** in the key of **A**
-     **A** to **E**   is a **IV-to-I** in the key of **E**

and so forth.

2.8.   In this way we arrive at the definitions of '**circle-of-fifths**' and '**circle-of-fourths**' as follows:-

-     *clockwise movement* around the circle results in a succession of **V-to-I** relationships - hence this direction is termed '**circle-of-fifths**'.
-     *counter-clockwise movement* around the circle results in a succession of **IV-to-I** relationships - hence this direction is termed '**circle-of-fourths**'.

This can be represented as follows:-

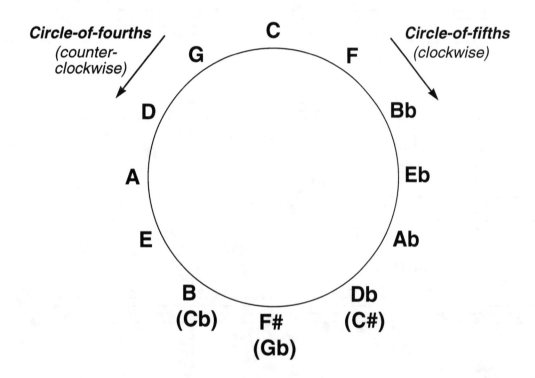

2.9.   As we said before - this may be a new way for you to approach the concept of 'circle-of-fifths' and 'circle-of-fourths'! I believe that this is the most productive interpretation for us at this point, for the following reasons:-

-     it neatly sidesteps the problems and potential confusion associated with deriving the 'circles' on an interval basis (as seen in **2.5.**)

-     most importantly, it *more accurately reflects how the ear works* as we hear progressions moving around the circle, as we will begin to see in the next chapter.

Chromatic Solfeg

3.1. In ***Contemporary Eartraining Level One*** we used diatonic solfeg syllables (**DO**, **RE**, **MI**, **FA**, **SO**, **LA**, and **TI**) to label the scale degrees of a major scale - see 'Level One Solfeg Review' on page 2 as necessary. This system is perfectly adequate for music which stays diatonic to a major key, which was our main focus in ***Level One***. However we now need to adapt the solfeg method to work with music that uses key changes, such as jazz tunes and more harmonically evolved contemporary styles. In adapting the solfeg system for these situations, we find that there are two possible approaches, which we will refer to as **Fixed 'DO'** and **Moveable 'DO'**. We can summarize these approaches as follows:-

- The **Moveable 'DO'** approach re-assigns **DO** to the tonic of each new key used in a piece of music, and then uses diatonic solfeg syllables within each new key. This would be suitable in certain contemporary styles where key changes are principally used for dramatic effect, and where the original key is not referenced thereafter (for example - all those pop ballads which modulate up a half-step!).
- The **Fixed 'DO'** approach keeps **DO** assigned to the tonic indicated by the original key signature, and treats any new keys used as **momentary key changes**. Extra solfeg syllables are therefore required to accommodate those tones which do not belong to the major scale of the key signature. This approach is suitable for jazz tunes and especially standards, where the melody is generally diatonic to the major scale of the key signature but where the harmony is routinely using chromatic tones and therefore implying momentary key changes.

3.2. Now we will consider an alteration to a **C** major scale (in the key of **C**), and interpret the results using both **Moveable 'DO'** and **Fixed 'DO'**. (Don't forget that **DO** could be any one of 12 pitches of course - this example starts with C major just for convenience). If we take a **C** major scale and then flat the note B (to become Bb), we get the following:-

(DO)

The **Moveable 'DO'** approach would recognize that we are no longer in the key of **C**, and that by flatting the note B to become Bb we have created an **F** major scale. We could then re-assign **DO** to F and retain the 'diatonic' solfeg syllables, as follows (see next page):-

3.2. contd.

SO   LA   TI   DO   RE   MI   FA   SO

3.3.   Now the **Fixed 'DO'** approach would keep **DO** assigned to C, and would recognize the alteration as evidence of a **momentary** key/scale change. However we will now need an additional syllable to represent Bb, as the 'flatted seventh' degree with respect to C as **DO**. The syllable for the flatted seventh degree is **TE** (pronounced TAY). So the **Fixed 'DO'** solution would be as follows:-

DO   RE   MI   FA   SO   LA   TE   (DO)

3.4.   Now we will consider the chromatic solfeg syllables for all other possible major scale alterations. These chromatic solfeg syllables have enharmonic equivalents in a similar fashion to the enharmonics existing between sharp and flat note names. For example, the notes C# and Db are the same pitch, but we would use one name or the other depending on the context i.e. whether we were actually sharping C or flatting D. Similarly, the chromatic pitches have alternate solfeg names depending on whether a diatonic pitch has been sharped or flatted. Here are all the syllables for the chromatic pitches, again assigning **DO** to C for the purposes of the example:-

DO DI RE RI MI FA FI SO SI LA LI TI (DO)

DO TI TE LA LE SO SE FA MI ME RE RA (DO)

FOR FURTHER INFORMATION ON CHROMATIC SOLFEG CONCEPTS, PLEASE REFER TO CHAPTER 4 OF OUR CONTEMPORARY MUSIC THEORY LEVEL 2 BOOK (SEE PAGE vii IN THIS BOOK).

3.5. The rules for creating these chromatic solfeg syllables can be summarized as follows:-

- ***Syllables for sharped pitches*** - Add the suffix 'I' (pronounced 'ee') after the first letter of the diatonic syllable being sharped i.e. **DO** becomes **DI**, **RE** becomes **RI**, etc.

- ***Syllables for flatted pitches*** - Add the suffix '**E**' (pronounced 'ay') after the first letter of the diatonic syllable being flatted i.e. **TI** becomes **TE**, **LA** becomes **LE**, etc. with the exception of **RE** which when flatted becomes **RA** (pronounced 'rah').

3.6. Now we can relate the earlier discussion concerning 'circle-of-fifths' and 'circle-of-fourths' (see Chapter 2) to the use of chromatic solfeg in a **Fixed 'DO'** environment. If **DO** was assigned to C, all the other keys around the circle could be represented via the use of chromatic solfeg as follows:-

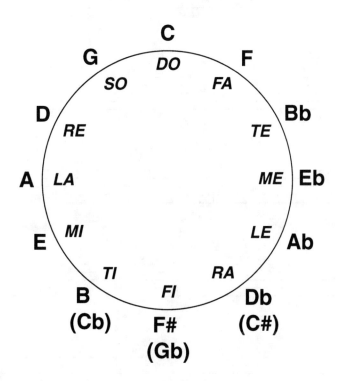

3.7. You may find it useful to refer to this diagram when working through the vocal drills which use **Fixed 'DO'** in Chapter 9. Again bear in mind that **DO** is assigned to C just for convenience - **DO** could have been assigned to any key around the circle.

Major triad progressions

4.1.　　　　First of all we will consider major triads moving around the circle-of-fifths and circle-of-fourths. We need to be able to distinguish between the **V-to-I** (circle-of-fifths) and **IV-to-I** (circle-of-fourths) types of movement - review Chapter 2 as required. These chordal movements are at the heart of many contemporary progressions and voiceleading structures. The method we will initially use to distinguish these movements is to consider how the individual tones are resolving within the chords used. We will do this by applying a **Moveable 'DO'** interpretation to 'pairs' of major triads which are 'voiceled' i.e. inverted to ensure a smooth connection between one chord and the next. In Chapter 2 we made the assumption that when moving around the circle, the triad we 'landed on' became the tonic of a new key. Continuing this concept, we will now take a closer look at the previously discussed **V-to-I** and **IV-to-I** triad movements.

4.2.　　　　This is how the individual tones will resolve on a **V-to-I** or circle-of-fifths type of motion (again remember that the last chord used represents the tonic of a new key - so **DO is assigned to F** in this case):-

Upper Voices:-

- **TI** resolves to **DO** (E to F in this example)
- **RE** resolves to **MI** (G to A in this example)
- **SO** is a commontone (C in this example)

Root voice:-

- **SO** resolves to **DO** (C to F in this example)

　　　　These solfeg movements (**TI** moving to **DO**, **RE** moving to **MI**, **SO** remaining common between the upper triads, and **SO** moving to **DO** in the bass voice) **will occur in all circle-of-fifths triad movements** irrespective of the inversions used, assuming that normal voiceleading techniques are applied.

4.3.　　　　Now we will look at how the individual tones will resolve on a **IV-to-I** or circle-of-fourths type of motion (again the last chord used represents the tonic of a new key - so **DO is assigned to G** in this case - see next page):-

4.3. contd.

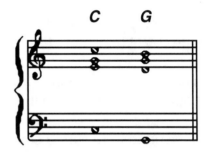

Upper Voices:-

- **FA** resolves to **MI** (C to B in this example)
- **LA** resolves to **SO** (E to D in this example)
- **DO** is a commontone (G in this example)

Root voice:-

- **FA** resolves to **DO** (C to G in this example)

In a similar manner to the circle-of-fifths progression, the above solfeg movements (**FA** moving to **MI**, **LA** moving to **SO**, **DO** remaining common between the upper triads, and **FA** moving to **DO** in the bass voice) <u>**will occur in all circle-of-fourths triad movements**</u> irrespective of the inversions used, again assuming that normal voiceleading techniques are applied.

4.4.   So how do we use these solfeg qualities to hear the difference between triads moving in circle-of-fifths and circle-of-fourths? Here are some techniques to work on:-

- The leading quality of the half-step (**TI to DO** or **FA to MI**) is a major indication. Listening for the direction of the half-step in the upper triad is an important technique.
- Hearing the top note of each triad voicing is another approach. This melodic line will normally be one of the active-to-resting solfeg resolutions (moving by half-step or whole-step, or maintaining a commontone).
- Listening for the commontone in the upper triad (either **SO** or **DO** of the key center) is another approach. The commontone will also be the root of the first or second chord respectively, within these major triad 'pairs'.
- Listening for the root voice (either **SO to DO** or **FA to DO**) is also important. The **SO** to **DO** movement will often sound more resolved due to the implied dominant-to-tonic relationship. (Note that the <u>**direction**</u> of the bass line, or whether it is a 4th or a 5th interval, is unimportant - both circle-of-fifths and circle-of-fourths movements can use 4th and 5th root intervals, moving up and/or down - see Chapter 2).
- For some people the sound of **V-to-I** implies a 'finality' and is a very 'leading' resolution, as opposed to the **IV-to-I** which is more 'unprepared' and less 'final'. Such impressions are subjective, but are arguably the result of recognizing the above individual resolutions in a more 'instinctive' manner.

4.5.   Now we will consider another type of movement between major triads in a progression - where the root moves by a half-step interval. We can relate these movements (together with those described earlier in this chapter) to our circle-of-fifths diagram as follows:-

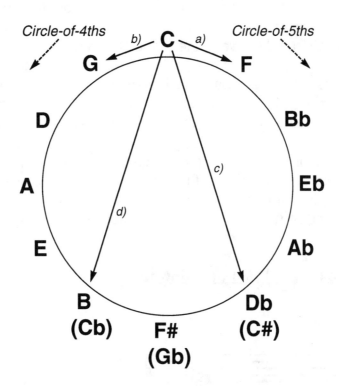

The labels **a)**, **b)**, **c)** & **d)** above refer to the following movements:-

- **a)**   Movement from C to F is **'circle-of-fifths'** (V-to-I)
- **b)**   Movement from C to G is **'circle-of-fourths'** (IV-to-I)
- **c)**   Movement from C to Db is **'half-step up'**
- **d)**   Movement from C to B is **'half-step down'**

4.6.   One reason why we are considering the half-step root interval at this stage, is that it is a very 'leading' and natural-sounding movement. These half-steps, together with the fourth and fifth root intervals previously discussed, are <u>**the root movements most easily understood by the ear**</u> and as such are a good starting point for us to begin transcribing triad progressions.

4.7.   First of all we need to be able to distinguish between the 'half-step' root interval and the 'circular' movements discussed in **4.1. - 4.4.** One approach to this can be derived from the circle diagram above. If each stage around the circle is considered as a new key center, then the further we travel from the top of the circle (C major in this case) the more altered the C major scale becomes in order to create the new scale required. In other words the distance

4.7. contd.

travelled on the circle can be used as a measure of the **degree of chromaticism** i.e. the degree to which the original scale has been altered. The circle-of-fifths and circle-of-fourths movements have a low degree of chromaticism, as we are only moving 'next door' on the circle - only one note has changed between the respective scales. Therefore these changes will sound very smooth and natural. Conversely, the half-step modulations have a high degree of chromaticism, as we are moving a substantial distance around the circle - the original major scale has been heavily altered. So these major triad movements will typically sound more 'chromatic' or 'abrupt' than the circular type of triad movements.

4.8. Another angle on distinguishing the half-step movements from the circular movements is to consider the 'parallel' aspects of the voiceleading. This is distinctly different from the voiceleading used for circular movement (see **4.2. - 4.3.**) which consists of different interval relationships as previously discussed. In the simplest case, all voices will move in parallel by half-step as follows:-

<u>a) Half-step up</u>   <u>b) Half-step down</u>

4.9. It is possible however for the voiceleading to apparently contradict the direction of this half-step movement. This is called 'opposite voiceleading' or contrary motion and can typically occur in a 'half-step up' change when moving from a root-position triad to a second-inversion triad, as follows:

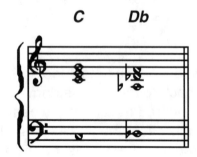

Note that the **C** triad is in root position while the **Db** triad is in 2nd inversion.

4.9. contd.

Also this can typically occur in a 'half-step down' change when moving from a second inversion triad to a root position triad, as follows:

Note that the **C** triad is in 2nd inversion while the **B** triad is in root position.

4.10. In order to avoid confusion when hearing these 'contrary motion' half-step situations it is important to focus on the direction of the root movement. If you are developing your awareness of the 'top note' of the voicing, the fact that the top note in the previous examples moves by whole-step (in the opposite direction to the root), may also be an important 'clue' in identifying the progression.

4.11. Now we will consider the combination of the movements discussed so far (circle-of-fifths, circle-of-fourths, half-step up, half-step down) into progressions. Remember that we are considering each stage on the circle as representing a new key center. Therefore progressions can always be considered as combinations of the relationships already discussed - in other words each 'pair' of chords in a progression can be isolated to determine whether it is a circle-of-fifths, circle-of-fourths, half-step up, or half-step down relationship. With this in mind, let us consider the following progression:-

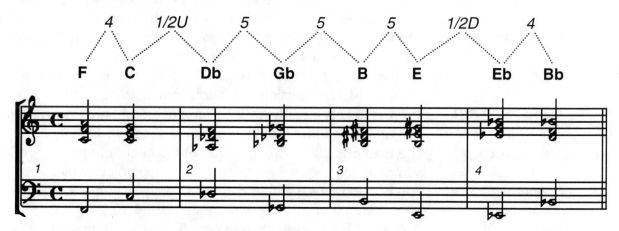

(Note that in this example the symbol '4' denotes circle-of-4ths, '5' denotes circle-of-5ths, '1/2U' denotes half-step up, and '1/2D' denotes half-step down).

4.11. contd.

This progression can be diagrammatically represented on the 'circle' as follows:-

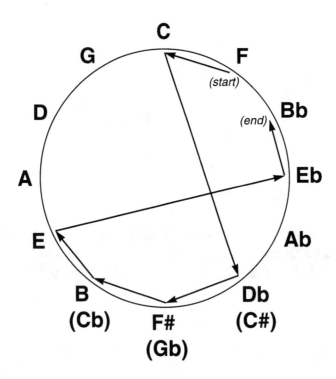

4.12.   This example combines all the allowable movements thus far:-

- Measure 1	- The **F** to **C** represents a circle-of-fourths movement with an implied **LA-SO** resolution in the top voiceleading.
- Measures 1 & 2	- The **C** to **Db** represents a half-step up movement, with 'contrary motion' voiceleading (see **4.9. - 4.10.**)
- Measure 2	- The **Db** to **Gb** represents a circle-of-fifths movement with an implied **TI-DO** resolution in the top voiceleading.
- Measures 2 & 3	- The **Gb** to **B** is a continuation of the circle-of-fifths movement, with an implied commontone of **SO** in the top voiceleading.
- Measure 3	- The **B** to **E** is also a continuation of the circle-of-fifths movement, with an impled **RE-MI** resolution in the top voiceleading.
- Measures 3 & 4	- The **E** to **Eb** represents a half-step down movement, again with 'contrary motion' voiceleading (see **4.9. - 4.10.**)
- Measure 4	- The **Eb** to **Bb** represents a circle-of-fourths movement with an implied commontone of **DO** in the top voiceleading.

4.13.   Notice that in the previous example we did not 'double back' on the circle i.e. no key center occurred more than once. The use of key center repetitions can enable a more complete 'contextual' view of a progression, as an alternative to simply viewing the progression as a series of 'pairs'. With this in mind, let us consider the following example:-

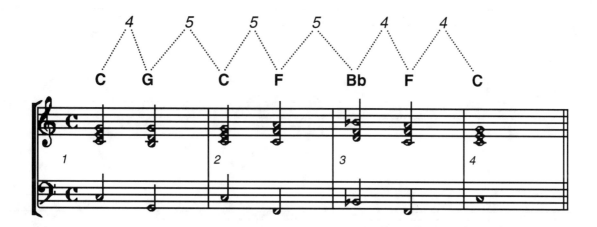

Again we can represent this diagrammatically as follows:-

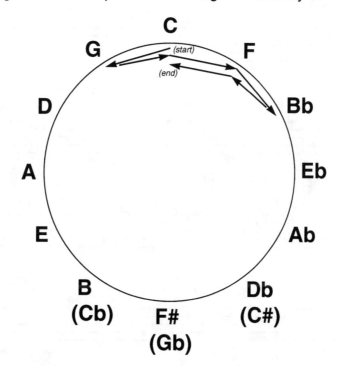

4.14.   In this example, the fact that C is used as the first, third and last chord in this progression can cause our ear to relate the progression to the key center of C. From this perspective, the progression could be viewed as a **I-V-I-IV-bVII-IV-I** in C. Alternately, the progression could still be considered as a succession of 'pairs' implying a new key center at each stage.

--- NOTES ---

22

Diatonic triad progressions

5.1.   This chapter is a continuation of the concepts first addressed in **Contemporary Eartraining Level 1**, where we learnt to recognize individual root-position diatonic triads and voiceled 'pairs' of diatonic triads. Now we will develop these methods further in order to hear four-chord diatonic progressions. Let us first review our concept of diatonic triads by considering the following example (key of C):

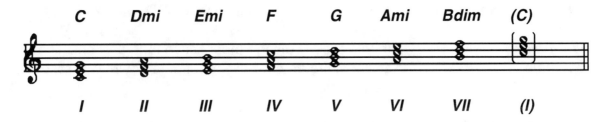

'Diatonic' simply means 'belonging to the scale' - the above chords are the result when we build triads from each scale degree and stay within the major scale restrictions. All diatonic progressions being considered here will always be in one key only - as opposed to the major triad progressions (see Chapter 4) which imply a new key center on each chord change. When working on these progressions, we will be hearing the root in the bass voice, and voiceled upper triads (in any inversion), in a similar fashion to the major triad progressions.

5.2.   The techniques used to hear these diatonic progressions can be summarized as
follows:-

- individual chord qualities
- active/resting qualities
- root movement
- commontones (or lack of) between successive chords
- voiceleading, especially top-note

5.3.   *INDIVIDUAL CHORD QUALITIES*

Here the choice will always be either a major, minor or diminished triad. The major and minor triads have strong and 'consonant' interval relationships. The major triad could be considered as having a 'bright', 'broad' or 'happy' impression while the minor triad could be considered as sounding 'dark', 'mellow', or 'sad' by comparison. Such impressions are of course subjective! The diminished triad by contrast has a more 'narrow' and 'dissonant' impression due to the presence of the tritone interval.

FOR FURTHER INFORMATION ON DIATONIC TRIADS AND PROGRESSIONS, PLEASE REFER TO CHAPTER 4 OF OUR CONTEMPORARY MUSIC THEORY LEVEL 1 BOOK, AND CHAPTER 6 OF OUR CONTEMPORARY MUSIC THEORY LEVEL 2 BOOK (SEE PAGE vii IN THIS BOOK).

5.4. _ACTIVE/RESTING QUALITIES_

5.4.1. Hearing the active and/or resting tones present in each diatonic triad can be an important clue. For example, let's say that at a certain point in a progression you heard a major triad. Using the active/resting tones could help you decide (i.e. between C, F or G major triads in the key of C) as follows:-

- _**I major**_
  (C major in key of C)
  - Always the most resting or resolved, due to the presence of all the resting tones **DO**, **MI** and **SO**.

- _**IV major**_
  (F major in key of C)
  - In this case **FA** is the most active tone present. The active half-step normally requires a downward resolution i.e. **FA-MI**.

- _**V major**_
  (G major in key of C)
  - In this case **TI** is the most active tone present. The active half-step normally requires an upward resolution i.e. **TI-DO**.

To summarize, hearing the upward or downward 'pull' of **TI** or **FA** can be an important technique to distinguish between the **IV** and **V** major triads.

5.4.2. Similar logic applies when distinguishing between the minor triads, as follows:-

- _**VI minor**_
  (A minor in key of C)
  - Always the most resting minor triad. **DO** and **MI** are fully resting tones and **LA** is only a semi-active tone (or 'active whole-step')

- _**II minor**_
  (D minor in key of C)
  - Similar comments as for the **IV** major. The presence of **FA** requires a downward resolution.

- _**III minor**_
  (E minor in key of C)
  - Similar comments as for the **V** major. The presence of **TI** requires an upward resolution.

5.4.3. Lastly, the VII diminished triad (B diminished in the key of C) will always sound the most active of all, due to the presence of both **TI** and **FA** in the chord.

5.5. _ROOT MOVEMENT_

5.5.1. The movements which occur between the roots of these diatonic triad progressions will consist of the following:-

- 'circular' 4th or 5th intervals i.e. implying a 'circle-of-fifths' or 'circle-of-fourths' type of motion.
- 'scalewise' implying 2 or more roots in succession either up or down the major scale, for example a **DO-RE-MI-FA** root movement.
- 'symmetric' implying the more non-leading root intervals of major and minor thirds and tritones.

5.5.2. The 'circular' type of root movement always has a very leading impression, hence the strength of the 'circle-of-fifths' and 'circle-of-fourths' types of progressions first seen in Chapter 4 - these movements can also occur within diatonic progressions of course. The 'scalewise' movement by comparison uses smaller intervals, and will sound melodic and natural as it is reinforcing the major scale of the key signature. The 'symmetric' movements are less leading and more difficult to hear, especially the tritone which is always the most 'angular' root movement encountered. Technically, symmetric root intervals result from dividing an octave into an equal number of parts i.e. tritones are created when dividing an octave by 2, thirds are created when dividing an octave by 3 or 4, etc. The most common 'symmetric' root movement in contemporary styles is the major or minor third interval.

5.6. _COMMONTONES BETWEEN CHORDS_

5.6.1. Hearing the commontones (or lack of) between successive diatonic chords can be very useful. Chord changes can be evaluated for their 'plurality', i.e. the tones which they may have in common. In these diatonic triad progressions, the most 'plural' chords will have 2 commontones between them, as in the following example:

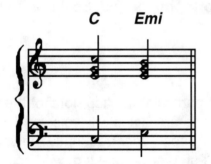

Here both **MI** and **SO** are commontones (assuming that C is **DO**)

The most 'plural' type of chord change in this diatonic setting (i.e. 2 commontones) **will always imply a root interval of a major or minor 3rd**. Further examples in the key of C would be **Dmi** to **F**, **Emi** to **G**, **F** to **Ami**, etc. So this 'maximum plurality' is an important clue in hearing this type of chord movement.

5.6.2.   In the next level down of plurality, successive chords will have one commontone between them, as in the following example:-

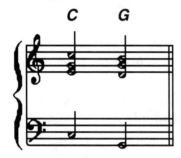

Here **SO** is a
commontone
(assuming that
C is **DO**)

Diatonic triad chord changes with one commontone will always either be a **'circular'** type of movment involving a root interval of a fourth or fifth, or a **'symmetric' tritone** root interval (for example B diminished to F in the key of C).

5.6.3.   In the lowest level of plurality, successive chords will have no commontones between them, as in the following example:

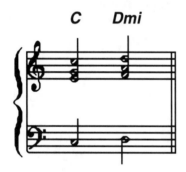

Here there are
no commontones
(everything is moving
by 'scalewise' steps)

Diatonic triad chord changes with no commontones will always be a 'scalewise' type of movement involving a **root interval of a major or minor 2nd**. So this is an important clue in hearing 'scalewise' chord movement.

5.7.   *VOICELEADING*

Hearing how the voiceleading works (in particular the 'top note' of the voicing) is another important angle. The great majority of contemporary styles will 'voicelead' from one chord to the next to give a more melodic and 'musical' effect. Very frequently the voiceleading (especially the 'top note') will be by commontone, half-step or whole-step, with occasional use of diatonic third intervals. The 'top-notes' of each successive chord will frequently function as a melodic line, with all the interval qualities and active/resting relationships that we would normally associate with a melody. Development of 'top-note' awareness is a major asset which we will continue to focus on in all subsequent Eartraining exercises.

5.8.   We will now consider some examples of four-chord diatonic progressions in the light of the various techniques available as above.

5.8.1.   *Diatonic triad progression example #1*

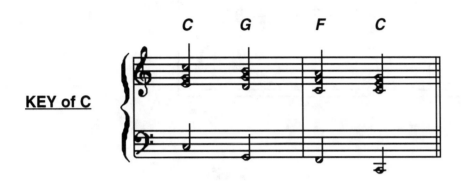

TECHNIQUE		**COMMENTS**
-	**Individual chord qualities**	- We hear all of these chords as having a major chord quality.
-	**Active/resting qualities**	- 1st chord: fully resting 2nd chord: has active tone **TI** 3rd chord: has active tone **FA** 4th chord: fully resting
-	**Root movement**	- 1st to 2nd chord: leading fourth interval implying circle-of-fourths type of motion - 2nd to 3rd chord: 'scalewise' whole-step - 3rd to 4th chord: another circle-of-fourths type movement
-	**Commontones**	- 1st to 2nd chord: one commontone (**SO**) implying 'circular' movement - 2nd to 3rd chord: no commontones, implying scalewise movement - 3rd to 4th chord: again one common tone (**DO**) implying 'circular' movement
-	**Top note voiceleading**	- the top notes of the voiceleading form the melodic line of **DO-TI-LA-SO**.

5.8.2.   *Diatonic triad progression example #2*

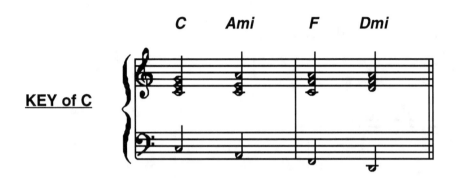

KEY of C

<u>TECHNIQUE</u>		<u>COMMENTS</u>
-	**Individual chord qualities**	- We hear the first and third chords as having a major quality and the second and fourth chords as having a minor quality.
-	**Active/resting qualities**	- 1st chord: fully resting 2nd chord: has semi-active tone **LA** but is still fairly resting overall 3rd chord: has active tone **FA** 4th chord: also has active tone **FA**
-	**Root movement**	- All the root movements are 'symmetric' diatonic third intervals.
-	**Commontones**	- All of the chord changes here are very 'plural' i.e. each change has the maximum of 2 commontones.
-	**Top note voiceleading**	- the top note moves from **SO** to **LA** on the first chord change. **LA** then stays on top for the remainder of the progression.

5.8.3. *Diatonic triad progression example #3*

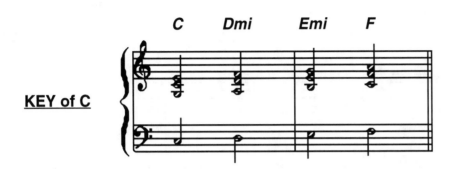

KEY of C

TECHNIQUE		COMMENTS
-	**Individual chord qualities**	- We hear the first and fourth chords as having a major quality and the second and third chords as having a minor quality.
-	**Active/resting qualities**	- 1st chord: fully resting 2nd chord: has active tone **FA** 3rd chord: has active tone **TI** 4th chord: has active tone **FA**
-	**Root movement**	- All the root movements are 'scalewise' resulting in the bass line of **DO-RE-MI-FA**.
-	**Commontones**	- There are no commontones between any pairs of successive chords. This is further evidence of the 'scalewise' nature of the bass line.
-	**Top note voiceleading**	- The top notes of the voiceleading form the melodic line of **MI-FA-SO-LA**.

Modal scale recognition

6.1.   As modal scales are so frequently used as melodic and harmonic sources in jazz and contemporary styles, it is appropriate that we now begin working on the recognition of these scales. Relating our ideas on modal scales to the earlier concepts of the 'circle-of-fifths', we will also see that key changes in a tune (which we can now begin to visualize on the 'circle') can be considered as modal alterations to the 'home-base' key or scale - in other words the recognition of the current modal scale being used, can help us to determine the key that a tune has modulated to - a valuable asset! In simple terms, a mode can be thought of as a 'displaced' major scale i.e. a major scale starting on a note other than the normal tonic or 'DO'. The following mode names are used depending upon the displacement of the major scale:-

SCALE DEGREE USED *IN BASS VOICE (TONIC)*		*MODE NAME*
II	*(i.e. D within a C major scale)*	*DORIAN*
III	*(i.e. E within a C major scale)*	*PHRYGIAN*
IV	*(i.e. F within a C major scale)*	*LYDIAN*
V	*(i.e. G within a C major scale)*	*MIXOLYDIAN*
VI	*(i.e. A within a C major scale)*	*AEOLIAN*
VII	*(i.e. B within a C major scale)*	*LOCRIAN*

6.2.   Using the above relationships, we can see for example that a C major scale starting on D would be **D Dorian**, a C major scale starting on E would be **E Phrygian**, etc. Now let's look at the modes from a different angle - what if we wanted to keep the same starting note (for example C) and to create the same modal scale relationships using this starting note? (i.e. a **Mixolydian** mode starting on C, a **Dorian** mode starting on C, etc.). In this case we would be **altering** the C major scale to create the modes required.

6.3.   Now we can relate these modal scale concepts to the circle-of-fifths (see diagram on next page):-

FOR FURTHER INFORMATION ON MODAL SCALES, PLEASE REFER TO CHAPTER 5 OF
OUR CONTEMPORARY MUSIC THEORY LEVEL 1 BOOK (SEE PAGE Vii IN THIS BOOK).

6.3. contd.

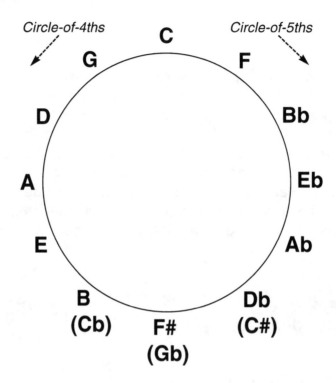

Circle-of-4ths   **C**   *Circle-of-5ths*

G   F

D   Bb

A   Eb

E   Ab

B (Cb)   F# (Gb)   Db (C#)

We recall from Chapter 4 that the further we moved from the home-base key (in this case **C** major) the more chromatic or altered the scale became. The **F** scale (next to C on the circle) has only one note different to the **C** scale (B is flatted to become Bb) as follows:

DO   **RE**   **MI**   **FA**   **SO**   **LA**   **TE**   **(DO)**

Using a **Fixed 'DO'** system, we needed the chromatic solfeg syllable '**TE**' for the altered tone of Bb - see Chapter 3. Notice that we have now created an **F** major scale starting from it's 5th degree - therefore this is effectively a <u>**C Mixolydian mode**</u>. So if we were able to recognize that the melodic/harmonic scale source of a tune had moved to C Mixolydian, this could be an effective short cut to detecting that a key change to **F Major** had occurred! Again this **Fixed 'DO'** example has **DO** assigned to C - **DO** however of course can be assigned to any key as required by the key signature of a tune.

6.4.   If we move one further stage round on the circle, we get to the key of **Bb**. Now we need a further alteration - E is flatted to become Eb, as follows (see next page):-

6.4. contd.

DO   RE   ME   FA   SO   LA   TE   (DO)

This is now a **Bb** major scale starting from it's second degree - therefore this is effectively a **C Dorian mode**. Again recognizing this mode being used, could be a useful short cut to detecting that a key change to **Bb major** had occurred.

6.5.   We can extend this idea to cover all major keys represented around the circle. It is desirable to represent all of these 'momentary' keys as alterations or 'modes' of the home-base key signature (in this case C major). However notice that in most keys on the 'sharp' (left-handed) side of the circle, the note C (or **DO** of the key signature) **itself requires alteration** i.e. these scales contain C# instead of C. So we can regard all keys around the circle as alterations to the 'home-base' scale, provided we include the modes in which the original tonic or **DO** (in this case C) has itself been altered. In this case we are therefore required to use some **C# modes** as well as **C modes**, to represent the keys on the 'sharp side', as follows:-

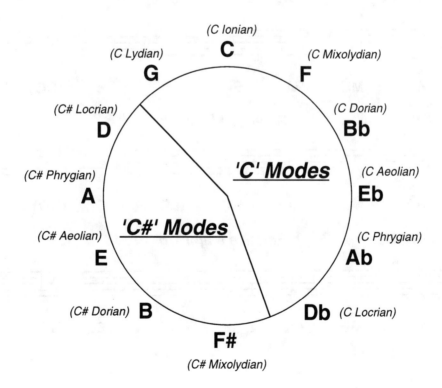

6.6. Starting at the top of the circle and moving clockwise (circle-of-fifths), here are the various modal scales (and 'momentary' key implications) produced:-

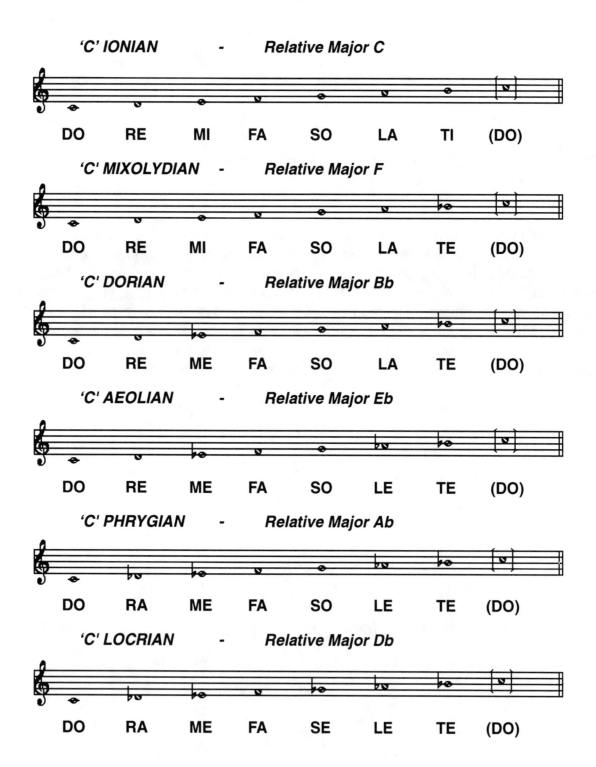

'C' IONIAN - *Relative Major C*

| DO | RE | MI | FA | SO | LA | TI | (DO) |

'C' MIXOLYDIAN - *Relative Major F*

| DO | RE | MI | FA | SO | LA | TE | (DO) |

'C' DORIAN - *Relative Major Bb*

| DO | RE | ME | FA | SO | LA | TE | (DO) |

'C' AEOLIAN - *Relative Major Eb*

| DO | RE | ME | FA | SO | LE | TE | (DO) |

'C' PHRYGIAN - *Relative Major Ab*

| DO | RA | ME | FA | SO | LE | TE | (DO) |

'C' LOCRIAN - *Relative Major Db*

| DO | RA | ME | FA | SE | LE | TE | (DO) |

6.6. contd.

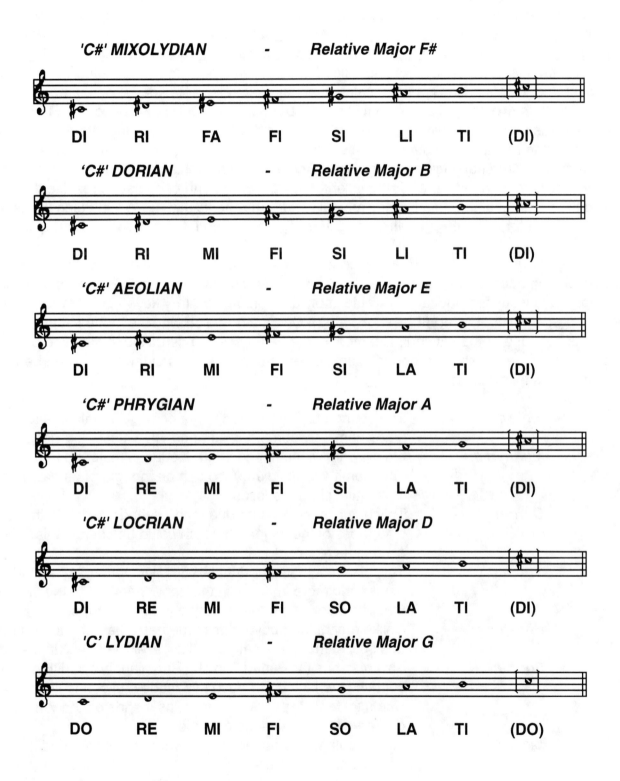

6.7. From an eartraining standpoint we need to be able to recognize each of these 12 modal scale relationships. Of course there are only seven modal scales, and most of these are duplicated (i.e. around the circle we have *C Phrygian* implying the key of *Ab*, and *C# Phrygian* implying the key of *A*, etc). <u>**Remember that we are doing this in order to represent (and therefore to hear) all possible momentary keys as modal alterations to the home-base scale!**</u> So with this goal in mind, we should try to hear even the C# modes as alterations to the home-base (i.e. in this case C major) scale, in the tape exercises provided. For example, *C# Locrian* only has two altered tones from C major (**DO** becomes **DI** and **FA** becomes **FI** - see 6.6.) and this is how we should try to hear it - however, the fact that one of the altered tones of the mode is also the starting note (i.e. C#) on the tape exercises, may make these 'C# mode' tape questions more challenging to begin with! Again, the goal in this case would be to detect a momentary key change to *D Major* (implied by *C# Locrian*), and of course in real life the tones in the mode could be used in any melodic and/or harmonic setting. When doing the tape exercises, listen for the <u>**solfeg quality**</u> of each mode, relative to **DO** (refer to 6.6. as required).

6.8. A further angle on hearing modal scales is to be aware of the interval relationships present in each mode. (To relate this to the above example quoting *C Phrygian* and *C# Phrygian* - as discussed above they would imply different momentary keys - but they would have the <u>**same vertical interval relationships**</u>). One main reason why the modes sound different is because of the varying placement of the half-steps. So detecting the leading quality of the half-steps becomes an important clue. Some interval attributes of the modes can be summarized as follows:-

-	***Ionian***	-	The sound of the unaltered major scale. Normal half-step placement between 3rd & 4th, and 7th & tonic degrees.
-	***Mixolydian***	-	Major scale with a flatted 7th. If it sounds major up to the 7th, then it's Mixolydian. Also can be thought of as having a 'dominant' characteristic.
-	***Dorian***	-	This has a 'minor' sound due to the flatted 3rd, but with the brightness of the major 6th which could be seen in this context as a 'color tone'.
-	***Aeolian***	-	This also has the 'minor' flatted 3rd like Dorian, but sounds darker and more 'mellow' in the upper part due to the flatted 6th. The Aeolian mode is also the natural minor scale.
-	***Phrygian***	-	Unlike any of the above, this mode has a flatted 2nd degree and so it starts with a half-step. However the 5th is unaltered.
-	***Locrian***	-	This also has the flatted 2nd like Phrygian, but additionally contains the flatted 5th. Also this mode can sound like it wants to 'resolve up' by half-step, as it ends on the 7th degree of the relative major scale.
-	***Lydian***	-	Major scale with a raised fourth, which gives this mode a 'bright' sounding impression. This is the only mode (apart from Ionian) which ends in a half-step.

II - V - I (two-five-one) progressions

7.1.   We will now begin our study of **II-V-I** progressions and how they relate to the circle-of-fifths. Our work in this area will involve the use of four-part chords - this is because the great majority of music using II-V-I progressions (jazz standards for example) uses these 'seventh chords' - typically ***IImi7 - V7 - Ima7***.

7.2.   The II-V-I progression is the most 'definitive' available within a key center. By this we mean that this progression most clearly defines the key center to our ear, due to the strong 'circle-of-fifths' root movement and the half-step movements between active and resting tones in the upper structure. See the following example:-

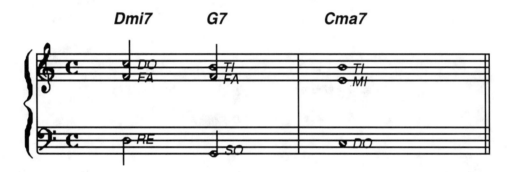

Notice that in this example we have only considered the root (in the bass clef) and the 3rd and 7th (in the treble clef) for each definitive chord. If we were to fully spell each four-part chord, each would have a perfect fifth above the root in the 'stack'. Therefore the fifth does not contribute towards our sense of chord quality or 'impression'. Also it is the movement between **FA-MI** and **DO-TI** in the upper structure which is really defining the scale and key center to our ear, and the fifth of each chord does not contribute in this respect either. It therefore follows that the ***root-3rd-7th*** or ***root-7th-3rd*** voicings are always the most economical and definitive for our purposes. We will use these voicings for all the II-V-I progressions at this point.

7.3.   In our previous discussion concerning major triad progressions around the circle-of-fifths (see Chapter 4) we saw that each stage around the circle could represent a new scale or 'momentary key'. It therefore follows that each stage around the circle could represent a II-V-I progression, as is demonstrated on the following page:-

For further information on II-V-I progressions, please refer to Chapter 2 of our Contemporary Music Theory Level 2 book (see page vii in this book).

7.3. contd.

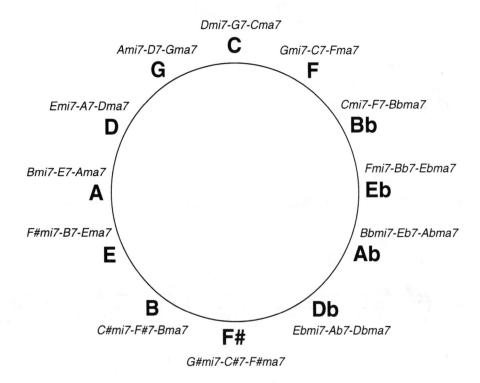

7.4. In a similar fashion to the major triad progressions around the circle (as seen in Chapter 4) we can now consider II-V-I four-part chord progressions around the circle. We will take the movements examined so far for major triads (circle-of-fifths, circle-of-fourths, half-step up, half-step down) and adapt them for II-V-I progressions as follows:-

- ***circle-of-fifths*** — this implies that we travel to the next clockwise key center on the circle i.e. ***Dmi7-G7-Cma7*** followed by ***Gmi7-C7-Fma7***.
- ***circle-of-fourths*** — this implies that we travel to the next counter-clockwise key center on the circle i.e. ***Dmi7-G7-Cma7*** followed by ***Ami7-D7-Gma7***.
- ***half-step up*** — this implies that the root of the I chord in the preceding key center moves up by half-step to the root of the II chord in the following key center i.e. ***Dmi7-G7-Cma7*** followed by ***C#mi7-F#7-Bma7***. *Note that the key center actually moves a half-step down (i.e. from **C** to **B**) in this case.*
- ***half-step down*** — this implies that the root of the I chord in the preceding key center moves down by half-step to the root of the II chord in the following key center i.e. ***Dmi7-G7-Cma7*** followed by ***Bmi7-E7-Ama7***. *Note that the key center actually moves a minor 3rd down (i.e. from **C** to **A**) in this case.*

7.5.   One further II-V-I modulation we will consider is known as 'root commontone'. In this case the root of the **I** chord in the preceding key center is the same as the root of the **II** chord in the following key center i.e. ***Dmi7-G7-Cma7*** followed by ***Cmi7-F7-Bbma7***. *Note that the key center actually moves a whole step down (i.e. from* __C__ *to* __Bb__*) in this case.*

7.6.   We can represent these possible movements diagrammatically on the circle-of-fifths as follows:-

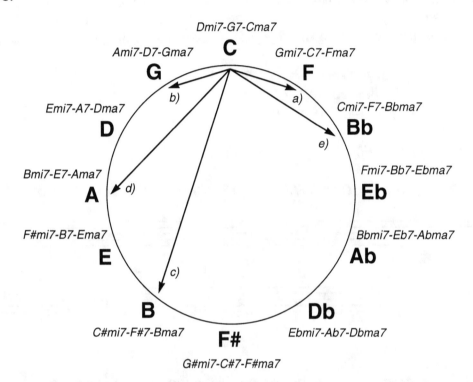

a)   -   Movement from key center of **C** to key center of **F** is **'circle-of-fifths'** (***Dmi7-G7-Cma7*** *moving to* ***Gmi7-C7-Fma7***)

b)   -   Movement from key center of **C** to key center of **G** is **'circle-of-fourths'** (***Dmi7-G7-Cma7*** *moving to* ***Ami7-D7-Gma7***)

c)   -   Movement from key center of **C** to key center of **B** is **'half-step up'** (***Dmi7-G7-Cma7*** *moving to* ***C#mi7-F#7-Bma7***)
        - again note that the term 'half-step up' refers to the root interval between the 1st **I** chord (Cma7 in this case) to the 2nd **II** chord (C#mi7 in this case).

d)   -   Movement from key center of **C** to key center of **A** is **'half-step down'** (***Dmi7-G7-Cma7*** *moving to* ***Bmi7-E7-Ama7***)
        - again note that the term 'half-step down' refers to the root interval between the 1st **I** chord (Cma7 in this case) to the 2nd **II** chord (Bmi7 in this case).

e)   -   Movement from key center of **C** to key center of **Bb** is **'root commontone'** (***Dmi7-G7-Cma7*** *moving to* ***Cmi7-F7-Bbma7***)
        - again note the term 'root commontone' refers to the same root used by the 1st **I** chord (Cma7 in this case) and the 2nd **II** chord (Cmi7 in this case).

7.7.   These five key changes collectively represent modulations with the lowest 'degree of chromaticism' (see **4.7.**) i.e. **'circle-of-fifths'** and **'circle-of-fourths'** where we have only moved to the next adjacent stage on the circle, or modulations using the most direct and leading root intervals between the keys, namely **'half-step up'**, **'half-step down'** and **'root commontone'** which use half-steps or a commontone in the root to connect the **I** chord of the first key to the **II** chord of the next key. As such these II-V-I key changes will occur very often in jazz tunes for example. We will now consider the individual characteristics of these five modulations more closely. In order to hear these progressions we will be focusing on three main techniques **as the I chord of the first key moves to the II chord of the second key**:-

- *root movement*
- *7-3 line voiceleading*
- *degree of chromaticism*

7.7.1.   <u>CIRCLE-OF-FIFTHS II-V-I key change</u>

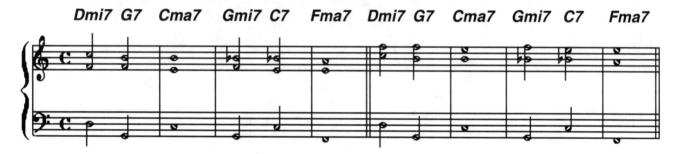

Dmi7 G7 Cma7   Gmi7 C7   Fma7   Dmi7 G7   Cma7   Gmi7 C7   Fma7

- Root movement	- The circle-of-fifths modulation always offers the strongest and most 'tonal' root movement available. The roots will always be moving by successive 4th and 5th intervals.
- 7-3 line voiceleading	- The circle-of-fifths modulation always offers 7-3 line voice-leading by half-step i.e. the 7th of the I chord moves down by half-step to the 3rd of the next II chord, and the 3rd of the I chord moves up by half-step to the 7th of the next II chord. This has a very melodic and 'leading' effect.
- Degree of chromaticism	- The circle-of-fifths modulation has a low degree of chromaticism as we are only moving to an adjacent stage on the circle - there is only a one-note difference between the respective implied scales. (However the chromatic tone to the first key - Bb in this case - is present in the II chord of the second key).

7.7.2. *CIRCLE-OF-FOURTHS II-V-I key change*

- ***Root movement***

  - The circle-of-fourths modulation has a (symmetric) minor 3rd root interval between the **I** chord and the following **II** chord. This rather 'non-leading' root interval is sometimes softened by the use of a 'descending 7th' bass line i.e. the root moving from C through B to A under the change **Cma7** to **Ami7**. However we should not rely on the presence of the 'descending 7th' when detecting this type of modulation.

- ***7-3 line voiceleading***

  - Here we have more options to consider than for circle-of-fifths, as indicated on the above examples a) - d). Example b) is the only situation offering half-step voiceleading in the top voice, with the 7th of the **I** chord moving up to the 3rd of the **II** chord. In all other cases the top-note voiceleading is by major or minor 3rd intervals.

- ***Degree of chromaticism***

  - As with circle-of-fifths, this modulation has a low degree of chromaticism as we are only moving to an adjacent stage on the circle. Also the following **II** chord is completely diatonic to the previous key center (i.e. **Ami7** in the key of **C**) which contributes to the 'plural' non-chromatic effect.

7.7.3.   *HALF-STEP UP II-V-I key change*

Dmi7 G7   Cma7 C#mi7 F#7   Bma7 Dmi7 G7   Cma7 C#mi7 F#7   Bma7

- **Root movement**   - The root movement between the **I** chord and the following **II** chord is the 'leading' half-step interval. Although strong and natural-sounding like the fourth and fifth root intervals, it of course has a far smaller interval span.

- **7-3 line voiceleading** - Here the important aspect to notice is that the 7-3 lines <u>**do not move**</u> between the **I** chord and the following **II** chord, i.e. they remain as commontones across the key change.

- **Degree of chromaticism** - The 'half-step up' modulation offers the greatest degree of chromaticism of all the modulations being considered, as we have effectively sharped five scale tones (i.e. going from the key of **C** to the key of **B** in this case). Referring to the circle diagram in **7.6.**, we note that the distance moved on the circle (a measure of the 'degree of chromaticism') is the greatest of all the key changes being studied.

7.7.4.   *HALF-STEP DOWN II-V-I key change*

- **Root movement**	- Comments as for half-step up (see **7.7.3.**)
- **7-3 line voiceleading**	- Here the 7-3 lines will normally voicelead down by whole-step, in a 'parallel' fashion (i.e. 7th down by whole step to 7th, and 3rd down by whole step to 3rd) between the **I** chord in the first key and the **II** chord in the second key.
- **Degree of chromaticism**	- The 'half-step down' modulation is fairly chromatic, as we have sharped three scale tones (i.e. going from the key of **C** to the key of **A** in this case). Again, refer to the circle diagram (in **7.6.**) as required.

7.7.5.   _ROOT COMMONTONE II-V-I key change_

- Root movement	- Here the important aspect to notice is that the root voice **does not move** between the **I** chord of the first key and the **II** chord of the second key i.e. it remains as a commontone acroos the key change.	
- 7-3 line voiceleading	- Here the 7-3 lines will normally voicelead down by half-step in a 'parallel' fashion (i.e. 7th down by half-step to 7th, 3rd down by half-step to 3rd) between the **I** chord in the first key and the **II** chord in the second key.	
- Degree of chromaticism	- The 'root commontone' modulation has a low-to-medium level of chromaticism. We have effectively flatted two scale tones (i.e. going from the key of **C** to the key of **Bb** in this case).	

7.8.   The above characteristics for II-V-I modulations can be summarized in the following table (again don't forget that the 'root movement' and '7-3 line voiceleading' comments refer to the movement between the **I** chord of the **1st** key and the **II** chord of the **2nd** key):-

	Root Movement	*7-3 Voiceleading*	*Degree Of Chromaticism*
CIRCLE-OF-5ths	Always leading, 'tonal' 4th and 5th intervals	Always by 'opposite' half-steps i.e. 3rd half-step up to 7th, 7th half-step down to 3rd	Low (Adjacent key on circle)
CIRCLE-OF-4ths	Non-leading 'symmetric' minor 3rd root interval (unless descending 7th is used)	7th up to 3rd offers half-step voiceleading. All other voiceleading is by major or minor 3rds	Low (Adjacent key on circle)
HALF-STEP UP	Leading, 'tonal' half-step root interval	7-3 lines **do not move** between I chord and following II chord	High (key signature altered by five sharps)
HALF-STEP DOWN	Leading, 'tonal' half-step root interval	Normally by 'parallel' whole steps i.e. 7th whole-step down to 7th, 3rd whole step down to 3rd	Medium to high (key signature altered by three sharps)
ROOT COMMON-TONE	Root voice **does not move** between I chord and following II chord	Normally by 'parallel' half-steps i.e. 7th half-step down to 7th, 3rd half-step down to 3rd	Low to medium (key signature altered by two flats)

The tape assignments in this area initially present 'pairs' of II-V-I progressions, followed by progressions with four key centers each. All key changes are within the above options.

7-3 melodic line dictation

8.1. We will now consider the 7-3 lines (i.e. the 7ths and 3rds of the chords) present in II-V-I progressions, from a melodic standpoint. We have already seen in Chapter 7 that the voiceleading of these 7-3 lines is a key component in understanding how II-V-I progressions move from one key to another. The 7ths and 3rds of these II-V-I chords also function well as melodic tones due to their 'definitive' character (see 7.2. text). For example, many standard tunes have melodies consisting of 7-3 lines over II-V-I harmonies, with some embellishment or 'passing' tones. We will first learn how to determine which 7-3 line is being used over a II-V-I progression. Then in situations where the 7-3 lines have been embellished with melodic passing tones, we will learn how to hear the inner 7-3 'skeleton' generally falling on the strong beats of the measure.

8.2. In the earlier study of II-V-I progressions we saw that there were two concurrent 7-3 lines occurring, as in the following example (*HS* = half-step, *CT* = commontone):-

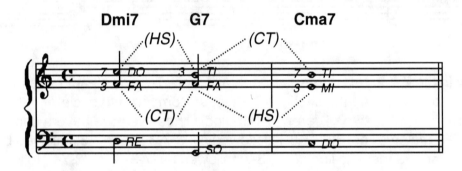

In the above example, the two concurrent 7-3 lines in the treble staff could be termed '7-3-7' and '3-7-3' respectively. Notice that the '7-3-7' line consists of a **half-step** followed by a **commontone** (**DO-TI-TI** of the key) and that the '3-7-3' line consists of a **commontone** followed by a **half-step** (**FA-FA-MI** of the key). Now we will look at how these melodic lines can be developed through II-V-I key changes around the circle-of-5ths and 4ths.

8.3. *7-3 melodic lines on II-V-I progressions moving around the circle-of-fifths*

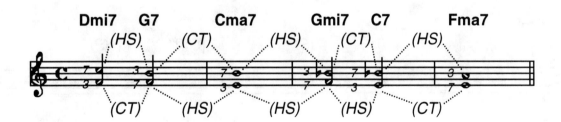

8.3. contd.   Because of the 'half-step' voiceleading between 7-3 lines going round the circle-of-5ths (as noted in **7.7.1.** text), the '7-3-7' and '3-7-3' lines may typically **alternate** during this type of key change. In other words, if the melody started out using the '7-3-7' line over the II-V-I in the key of **C**, it could then typically lead to the '3-7-3' line over the II-V-I in **F**, and so on.

8.4.   *7-3 melodic lines on II-V-I progressions moving around the circle-of-fourths*

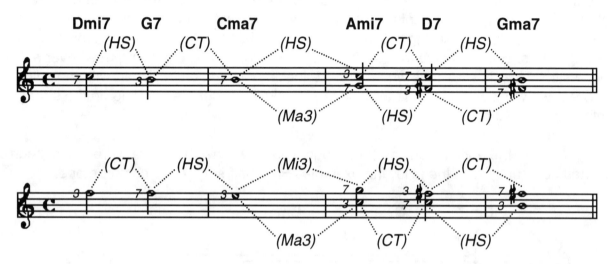

        As we saw in the **7.7.2.** text, there are generally more 7-3 voiceleading options for the II-V-I progression moving around the circle-of-fourths, as compared to circle-of-fifths. Each staff above therefore illustrates **two different** 7-3 melodic lines. Now we have a choice between alternating the 7-3 melodic lines i.e. '7-3-7' followed by '3-7-3', or '3-7-3' followed by '7-3-7', or repeating the same 7-3 melodic line i.e. '7-3-7' followed by '7-3-7', or '3-7-3' followed by '3-7-3'. Note that major or minor 3rd melodic intervals occur between the keys, in three out of the four melodic options shown above.

8.5.   We will now consider how embellishments or 'passing tones' can be added to these 7-3 line melodies round the circle-of-fifths and circle-of-fourths. For now, we will work within the restrictions of keeping the 7-3 definitive tones on the strong beats. If each II-V-I progression occupies two measures, then for our purposes here the strong beats would be considered to be beat 1 of the first measure (where the **II** chord would land), beat 3 of the first measure (where the **V** chord would land) and beat 1 of the second measure (where the **I** chord would land). Consider the following circle-of-fifths example:-

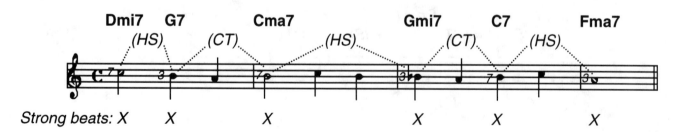

Strong beats: X   X   X   X   X   X

8.5.　　　　Listening to the tones on the strong beats, we can listen for the half-step followed by the commontone in the melody over the first II-V-I progression, which tells us that a '7-3-7' line is being used. (We can alternatively detect the solfeg quality of **DO-TI-TI**, with respect to the key of **C**, being used in the melody). We can listen for the commontone followed by the half-step in the melody over the second II-V-I progression, which tells us that a '3-7-3' line is being used. (We can alternatively detect the solfeg quality of **FA-FA-MI**, with respect to the key of **F**, being used in the melody). Finally in order to hear that the II-V-I progressions are moving in a circle-of-fifths manner, in addition to the techniques covered in **7.7.1.** we can listen for the 7th in the melody on the **Cma7** (B) move **down by half-step** to the 3rd on the **Gmi7** (Bb), as in the top melody line shown in **8.3.** Having derived this 7-3 'skeleton' or underlying structure of the melody, we can then listen for the passing or embellishment tones added in the melody on the weak beats. On the tape exercises these will generally be diatonic scale steps adjacent to the 7-3 lines.

8.6.　　　　Now we will consider a circle-of-fourths example, again using 'passing tones' in the melody between the strong beats.

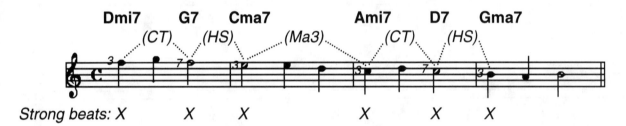

Strong beats: X　　　　X　　X　　　　X　　X　　X

8.7.　　　　Listening to the tones on the strong beats, we can listen for the commontone followed by the half-step in the melody over the first II-V-I progression, which tells us that a '3-7-3' line is being used. (We can alternatively detect the solfeg quality of **FA-FA-MI**, with respect to the key of **C**, being used in the melody). We can again listen for the commontone followed by the half-step in the melody over the second II-V-I progression, which tells us that another '3-7-3' line is being used. In order to hear that the II-V-I progressions are moving in a circle-of-fourths manner, in addition to the techniques covered in **7.7.2.** we can listen for the 3rd in the melody on the **Cma7** (E) move **down by major 3rd** to the 3rd on the **Ami7** (C), as in the bottom melody line shown on the second staff in **8.4.** This larger melodic voiceleading interval across the key change of a 3rd, and the repetition of the '3-7-3' line on each key, would be evidence of 'circle-of-fourths' rather than 'circle-of-fifths' movement between these II-V-I progressions. Again having derived the 7-3 'skeleton' or underlying structure of the melody, we can then listen for the passing or embellishment tones added on the weak beats.

8.8.　　　　The tape assignments start out with 7-3 melodies using the options shown in **8.3.** and **8.4.** across 2 key centers, and then across 4 key centers (maintaining a circle-of-5ths or 4ths direction for each progression). In the last section, melodic passing tones are added, again across 2 keys and then 4 keys, along the lines shown in **8.5.** and **8.6.**

Vocal drills

The following vocal drills will help reinforce the concepts presented so far. If you are using the cassette tapes which are available, these drills are included on **Tape 1 Side A**.

9.1.   *Vocal drill #1 - Circle-of-fifths using Moveable 'DO'*

9.2. *Vocal drill #2 - Circle-of-fifths using Fixed 'DO'*

9.3. _Vocal drill #3 - Circle-of-fourths using Moveable 'DO'_

9.4. *Vocal drill #4 - Circle-of-fourths using Fixed 'DO'*

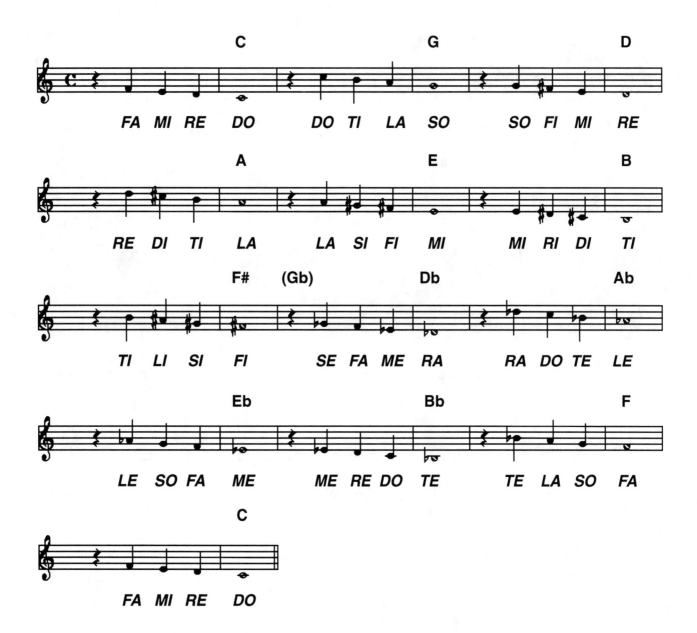

9.5. *Vocal drill #5 - Roots of II - V - I progressions around circle-of-5ths using Fixed 'DO'.*

9.5. *Vocal drill #6 - Roots of II - V - I progressions around circle-of-4ths using Fixed 'DO'.*

(You may optionally sing 'descending 7ths' as indicated).

9.5. _Vocal drill #7 - 7-3 lines generated by II-V-I progressions around circle-of-5ths using Fixed 'DO'._

Contents of cassette tapes which are available (see page vi)

Tape no.	Side		Contents	
1	**A**	-	*Major triad progressions - pairs*	
			- textbook	p15-22
			- workbook questions	p62-63
			- workbook answers	p90-92
		-	*Major triad progressions - three chords each*	
			- textbook	p15-22
			- workbook questions	p64-65
			- workbook answers	p93-97
		-	*Vocal drills*	
			- textbook	p51-58
1	**B**	-	*Major triad progressions - four and eight chords each*	
			- textbook	p15-22
			- workbook questions	p66-68
			- workbook answers	p98-115
2	**A**	-	*Diatonic triad progressions*	
			- textbook	p23-30
			- workbook questions	p69-71
			- workbook answers	p116-127
2	**B**	-	*Modal scales*	
			- textbook	p31-36
			- workbook questions	p72-74
			- workbook answers	p128-129
		-	*II-V-I progressions - pairs*	
			- textbook	p37-46
			- workbook questions	p75-76
			- workbook answers	p130-135

(continued on next page>>>)

Contents of cassette tapes which are available (contd)

Tape no.	Side		Contents
3	*A*	-	*II-V-I progressions - four key centers each*

- textbook p37-46
- workbook questions p77-78
- workbook answers p136-146

- *7-3 melodic line dictation with harmonization*
  (7-3 lines **only** in melodies - questions 1-30)
  - textbook p47-50
  - workbook questions p79-83
  - workbook answers p147-150

| *3* | *B* | - | *7-3 melodic line dictation with harmonization* |

(passing tones added in melodies - questions 31-60)
- textbook p47-50
- workbook questions p79, & p84-87
- workbook answers p151-154

Note to students - if you are doing the Eartraining exercises, the Workbook Questions section is where you write your answers. If you are studying with an instructor, they can use the Workbook Answers section as a source of questions - otherwise you can do the exercises on a self-study basis using the cassette tapes which are available (see page *vi*).

Note to teachers - if you are drilling students on this material, you can play from the Workbook Answers section, and the students can fill out their answers here.

This part of the book contains questions and instructions on the following areas:-

1.   Major triad progressions - 'pairs' (two chords each)

2.   Major triad progressions - three chords each

3.   Major triad progressions - four and eight chords each

4.   Diatonic triad progressions

5.   Modal scales

6.   II-V-I progressions - 'pairs' (two key centers each)

7.   II-V-I progressions - four key centers each

8.   7-3 melodic line dictation with harmonization

Please refer back to the relevant chapters in the textbook as necessary as you work through these exercises.

1. <u>*MAJOR TRIAD PROGRESSIONS - PAIRS*</u>

The following pairs of voiceled major triads will be moving in one of the following ways:-

- circle-of-fifths

- circle-of-fourths

- half-step up

- half-step down

You are to determine which of these possibilities is being played for each question (the abbreviations **5**, **4**, **1/2U**, or **1/2D** are acceptable).

Questions 1 - 25 will consist of only circle-of-fifths or circle-of-fourths movements.

Questions 26-50 will use all the various possibilities listed above.

Write your answers here:-

1. _____
2. _____
3. _____
4. _____
5. _____
6. _____
7. _____
8. _____
9. _____
10. _____
11. _____
12. _____
13. _____
14. _____
15. _____
16. _____
17. _____
18. _____
19. _____
20. _____
21. _____
22. _____
23. _____
24. _____
25. _____

26. _____
27. _____
28. _____
29. _____
30. _____
31. _____
32. _____
33. _____
34. _____
35. _____
36. _____
37. _____
38. _____
39. _____
40. _____
41. _____
42. _____
43. _____
44. _____
45. _____
46. _____
47. _____
48. _____
49. _____
50. _____

2.   *MAJOR TRIAD PROGRESSIONS - THREE CHORDS EACH*

The movements between the chords in these three-chord progressions are again restricted to either circle-of-fifths, circle-of-fourths, half-step up or half-step down.

You are to determine which two of these possibilities are being played for each question (again the abbreviations **5**, **4**, **1/2U** or **1/2D** are acceptable).

64

Write your answers here:-

1. _____ followed by _____
2. _____ followed by _____
3. _____ followed by _____
4. _____ followed by _____
5. _____ followed by _____
6. _____ followed by _____
7. _____ followed by _____
8. _____ followed by _____
9. _____ followed by _____
10. _____ followed by _____
11. _____ followed by _____
12. _____ followed by _____
13. _____ followed by _____
14. _____ followed by _____
15. _____ followed by _____
16. _____ followed by _____
17. _____ followed by _____
18. _____ followed by _____
19. _____ followed by _____
20. _____ followed by _____
21. _____ followed by _____
22. _____ followed by _____
23. _____ followed by _____
24. _____ followed by _____
25. _____ followed by _____

26. _____ followed by _____
27. _____ followed by _____
28. _____ followed by _____
29. _____ followed by _____
30. _____ followed by _____
31. _____ followed by _____
32. _____ followed by _____
33. _____ followed by _____
34. _____ followed by _____
35. _____ followed by _____
36. _____ followed by _____
37. _____ followed by _____
38. _____ followed by _____
39. _____ followed by _____
40. _____ followed by _____
41. _____ followed by _____
42. _____ followed by _____
43. _____ followed by _____
44. _____ followed by _____
45. _____ followed by _____
46. _____ followed by _____
47. _____ followed by _____
48. _____ followed by _____
49. _____ followed by _____
50. _____ followed by _____

3. *MAJOR TRIAD PROGRESSIONS - FOUR and EIGHT CHORDS EACH*

The movements between the chords in these four-chord and eight-chord progressions are again restricted to either circle-of-fifths, circle-of-fourths, half-step up or half-step down.

In each case the starting triad (chord symbol) is shown in the first box. Please write the remaining chord symbols in the empty boxes for each progression.

Questions 1 - 8 and 26 - 33 will consist of either circle-of-fifths only or circle-of-fourths only, with no other movements.

Questions 9 - 16 and 34 - 41 will consist of circle-of-fifths and circle-of-fourths movements, with one 'change of direction' occurring around the circle.

Questions 17 - 25 and 42 - 50 will consist of circle-of-fifths and/or circle-of-fourths movements, and will additionally contain one half-step movement (up or down).

Questions 51 - 100 will freely combine all allowable movements.

(As an optional extra assignment, you may work on transcribing the voicings used in these progressions. All voicings used on the tapes are printed for your reference in the Workbook Answers section of the book).

Write your answers here:-

No.					No.								
1.	C				26.	F							
2.	F				27.	Bb							
3.	Bb				28.	Eb							
4.	Eb				29.	Ab							
5.	Ab				30.	Db							
6.	Db				31.	F#							
7.	F#				32.	B							
8.	B				33.	E							
9.	E				34.	A							
10.	A				35.	D							
11.	D				36.	G							
12.	G				37.	C							
13.	C				38.	F							
14.	F				39.	Bb							
15.	Bb				40.	Eb							
16.	Eb				41.	Ab							
17.	Ab				42.	Db							
18.	Db				43.	F#							
19.	F#				44.	B							
20.	B				45.	E							
21.	E				46.	A							
22.	A				47.	D							
23.	D				48.	G							
24.	G				49.	C							
25.	C				50.	F							

(contd. from previous page)

51.	Bb			
52.	Eb			
53.	Ab			
54.	Db			
55.	F#			
56.	B			
57.	E			
58.	A			
59.	D			
60.	G			
61.	C			
62.	F			
63.	Bb			
64.	Eb			
65.	Ab			
66.	Db			
67.	F#			
68.	B			
69.	E			
70.	A			
71.	D			
72.	G			
73.	C			
74.	F			
75.	Bb			

76.	Eb							
77.	Ab							
78.	Db							
79.	F#							
80.	B							
81.	E							
82.	A							
83.	D							
84.	G							
85.	C							
86.	F							
87.	Bb							
88.	Eb							
89.	Ab							
90.	Db							
91.	F#							
92.	B							
93.	E							
94.	A							
95.	D							
96.	G							
97.	C							
98.	F							
99.	Bb							
100.	Eb							

4.   *DIATONIC TRIAD PROGRESSIONS*

You are to provide chord symbols for the following four-chord voiceled diatonic triad progressions. In each case the key of each progression is indicated to the left of the first box.

Questions 1 - 25 are in the key of C and start with the I chord (i.e. C major).

Questions 26 - 50 are also in the key of C but do not necessarily start with the I triad.

Questions 51 - 75 are in keys other than C and start with the I triad in the respective key.

Questions 76 - 100 are also in keys other than C and do not necessarily start with the I triad in the respective key.

In each case **DO** of the respective key center is given as a reference tone beforehand.

(As an optional extra assignment, you may work on transcribing the voicings used in these progressions. All voicings used on the tapes are printed for your reference in the Workbook Answers section of the book).

Write your answers here:-

#	Key	C			
1.	Key of C	C			
2.	Key of C	C			
3.	Key of C	C			
4.	Key of C	C			
5.	Key of C	C			
6.	Key of C	C			
7.	Key of C	C			
8.	Key of C	C			
9.	Key of C	C			
10.	Key of C	C			
11.	Key of C	C			
12.	Key of C	C			
13.	Key of C	C			
14.	Key of C	C			
15.	Key of C	C			
16.	Key of C	C			
17.	Key of C	C			
18.	Key of C	C			
19.	Key of C	C			
20.	Key of C	C			
21.	Key of C	C			
22.	Key of C	C			
23.	Key of C	C			
24.	Key of C	C			
25.	Key of C	C			

26.	Key of C				
27.	Key of C				
28.	Key of C				
29.	Key of C				
30.	Key of C				
31.	Key of C				
32.	Key of C				
33.	Key of C				
34.	Key of C				
35.	Key of C				
36.	Key of C				
37.	Key of C				
38.	Key of C				
39.	Key of C				
40.	Key of C				
41.	Key of C				
42.	Key of C				
43.	Key of C				
44.	Key of C				
45.	Key of C				
46.	Key of C				
47.	Key of C				
48.	Key of C				
49.	Key of C				
50.	Key of C				

70

(contd from previous page)

51.	Key of G	**G**			
52.	Key of D	**D**			
53.	Key of A	**A**			
54.	Key of E	**E**			
55.	Key of B	**B**			
56.	Key of F#	**F#**			
57.	Key of Db	**Db**			
58.	Key of Ab	**Ab**			
59.	Key of Eb	**Eb**			
60.	Key of Bb	**Bb**			
61.	Key of F	**F**			
62.	Key of Bb	**Bb**			
63.	Key of Eb	**Eb**			
64.	Key of Ab	**Ab**			
65.	Key of Db	**Db**			
66.	Key of F#	**F#**			
67.	Key of B	**B**			
68.	Key of E	**E**			
69.	Key of A	**A**			
70.	Key of D	**D**			
71.	Key of G	**G**			
72.	Key of D	**D**			
73.	Key of A	**A**			
74.	Key of E	**E**			
75.	Key of Cb	**Cb**			

76.	Key of Gb				
77.	Key of C#				
78.	Key of Ab				
79.	Key of Eb				
80.	Key of Bb				
81.	Key of F				
82.	Key of Bb				
83.	Key of Eb				
84.	Key of Ab				
85.	Key of C#				
86.	Key of Gb				
87.	Key of Cb				
88.	Key of E				
89.	Key of A				
90.	Key of D				
91.	Key of G				
92.	Key of D				
93.	Key of A				
94.	Key of E				
95.	Key of B				
96.	Key of F#				
97.	Key of Db				
98.	Key of Ab				
99.	Key of Eb				
100.	Key of Bb				

5.   *MODAL SCALES*

You are to identify the following modal scales.

Questions 1 - 25 will consist of modes starting on 'C', from the following possibilities:-

-     C Ionian
-     C Mixolydian
-     C Dorian
-     C Aeolian
-     C Phrygian
-     C Locrian
-     C Lydian

Questions 26 - 50 will consist of modes starting on 'C#', from the following possibilities:-

-     C# Mixolydian
-     C# Dorian
-     C# Aeolian
-     C# Phrygian
-     C# Locrian

Questions 51 - 100 will freely mix all the above possibilities.

For all questions a mode description (i.e. Dorian, Phrygian etc.) and a relative or implied major scale, are required. Additionally for **questions 51 - 100** you are to determine whether the mode starts on C or C#.

In each case Middle C (**DO**) is given as a reference tone beforehand.

72

Write your answers here:-

	Starting note	Mode description	Relative major			Starting note	Mode description	Relative major
1.	C				26.	C#		
2.	C				27.	C#		
3.	C				28.	C#		
4.	C				29.	C#		
5.	C				30.	C#		
6.	C				31.	C#		
7.	C				32.	C#		
8.	C				33.	C#		
9.	C				34.	C#		
10.	C				35.	C#		
11.	C				36.	C#		
12.	C				37.	C#		
13.	C				38.	C#		
14.	C				39.	C#		
15.	C				40.	C#		
16.	C				41.	C#		
17.	C				42.	C#		
18.	C				43.	C#		
19.	C				44.	C#		
20.	C				45.	C#		
21.	C				46.	C#		
22.	C				47.	C#		
23.	C				48.	C#		
24.	C				49.	C#		
25.	C				50.	C#		

(contd. from previous page)

	Starting note	Mode description	Relative major		Starting note	Mode description	Relative major
51.				76.			
52.				77.			
53.				78.			
54.				79.			
55.				80.			
56.				81.			
57.				82.			
58.				83.			
59.				84.			
60.				85.			
61.				86.			
62.				87.			
63.				88.			
64.				89.			
65.				90.			
66.				91.			
67.				92.			
68.				93.			
69.				94.			
70.				95.			
71.				96.			
72.				97.			
73.				98.			
74.				99.			
75.				100.			

6.   *II-V-I PROGRESSIONS - PAIRS*

The following progressions consist of two II-V-I sequences in different keys. In each case the movement from the first to the second key center is restricted to the following possibilities:-

- circle-of-fifths
- circle-of-fourths
- half-step up
- half-step down
- root commontone

Note that in this context, the terms 'circle-of-fifths' and 'circle-of-fourths' refer to the relationship between the successive key centers, whereas the terms 'half-step up', 'half-step down' and 'root commontone' refer to the interval between the root of the I chord in the first key center and the root of the II chord in the second key center (see Chapter 7 text).

You are to determine which of these possibilities is being played for each question (the abbreviations **5**, **4**, **1/2U**, **1/2D** or **RC** are acceptable).

Questions 1 - 10 will start in the key center of C and will consist only of circle-of-fifths or circle-of-fourths movements.

Questions 11 - 25 will use all possible starting keys and will again consist only of circle-of-fifths or circle-of-fourths movements.

Questions 26 - 35 will start in the key center of C and will contain any of the allowable movements (i.e. circle-of-fifths, circle-of-fourths, half-step up, half-step down and root commontone).

Questions 36 - 50 will use all possible starting keys and allowable movements as above.

Write your answers here:-

1.	_____	26.	_____
2.	_____	27.	_____
3.	_____	28	_____
4.	_____	29.	_____
5.	_____	30.	_____
6.	_____	31.	_____
7.	_____	32.	_____
8.	_____	33.	_____
9.	_____	34.	_____
10.	_____	35.	_____
11.	_____	36.	_____
12.	_____	37.	_____
13.	_____	38.	_____
14.	_____	39.	_____
15.	_____	40.	_____
16.	_____	41.	_____
17.	_____	42.	_____
18.	_____	43.	_____
19.	_____	44.	_____
20.	_____	45.	_____
21.	_____	46.	_____
22.	_____	47.	_____
23.	_____	48.	_____
24.	_____	49.	_____
25.	_____	50.	_____

7. *II-V-I PROGRESSIONS - FOUR KEY CENTERS EACH*

The following progressions consist of four II-V-I sequences in different keys. The movements between the key centers are again restricted to circle-of-fifths, circle-of-fourths, half-step up, half-step down, or root commontone.

In each case the starting key center is shown in the first box. Please write the remaining **key centers** in the empty boxes for each progression (review the key center implications of each possible movement on pages 38-39 as necessary).

Questions 1 - 25 will all start in the key center of C major.

Questions 26 - 50 will use all 12 possible starting key centers.

(As an optional extra assignment, you may work on transcribing the voicings used in these progressions. All voicings used on the tapes are printed for your reference in the Workbook Answers section of the book).

Write your answers here:-

#				
1.	C			
2.	C			
3.	C			
4.	C			
5.	C			
6.	C			
7.	C			
8.	C			
9.	C			
10.	C			
11.	C			
12.	C			
13.	C			
14.	C			
15.	C			
16.	C			
17.	C			
18.	C			
19.	C			
20.	C			
21.	C			
22.	C			
23.	C			
24.	C			
25.	C			

#				
26.	F			
27.	Bb			
28.	Eb			
29.	Ab			
30.	Db			
31.	F#			
32.	B			
33.	E			
34.	A			
35.	D			
36.	G			
37.	C			
38.	F			
39.	Bb			
40.	Eb			
41.	Ab			
42.	C#			
43.	Gb			
44.	Cb			
45.	E			
46.	A			
47.	D			
48.	G			
49.	C			
50.	F			

8. *7-3 MELODIC LINE DICTATION WITH HARMONIZATION*

You are to supply chord symbols above the staff, and melody notes on the staff, for the following 4-measure and 8-measure examples.

The harmonization will consist of II-V-I sequences moving in either a circle-of-fifths or circle-of-fourths fashion. In each case the starting II-V-I progression is indicated above the first 2 measures.

Questions 1 - 30 will only contain 7-3 lines in the melody, with no additional passing tones.

Questions 31 - 60 will contain diatonic passing tones in addition to 7-3 lines in the melody.

Don't forget to include any necessary accidentals (sharps and flats) in the melodies.

Write your answers here:-

1. **Dmi7 / G7 / Cma7 / / /**

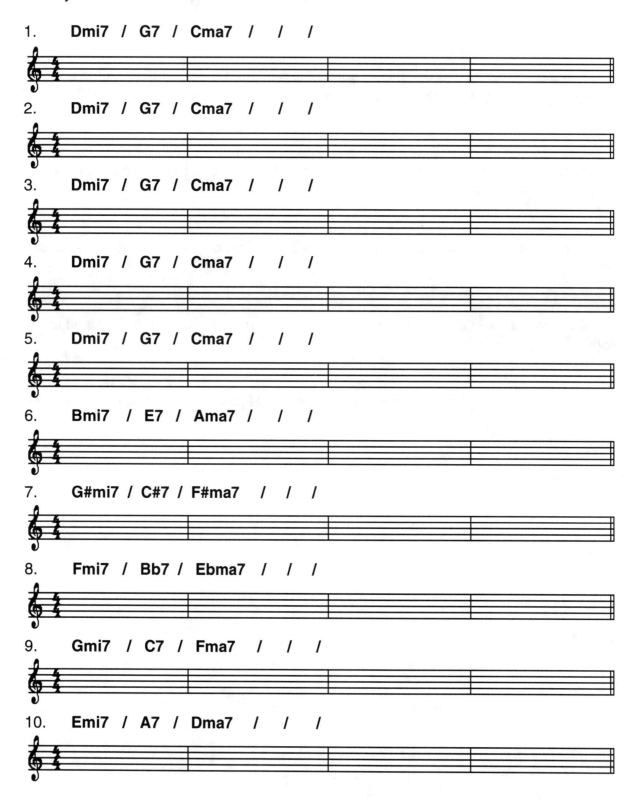

2. **Dmi7 / G7 / Cma7 / / /**

3. **Dmi7 / G7 / Cma7 / / /**

4. **Dmi7 / G7 / Cma7 / / /**

5. **Dmi7 / G7 / Cma7 / / /**

6. **Bmi7 / E7 / Ama7 / / /**

7. **G#mi7 / C#7 / F#ma7 / / /**

8. **Fmi7 / Bb7 / Ebma7 / / /**

9. **Gmi7 / C7 / Fma7 / / /**

10. **Emi7 / A7 / Dma7 / / /**

(contd)

11. **C#mi7 / F#7 / Bma7 / / /**

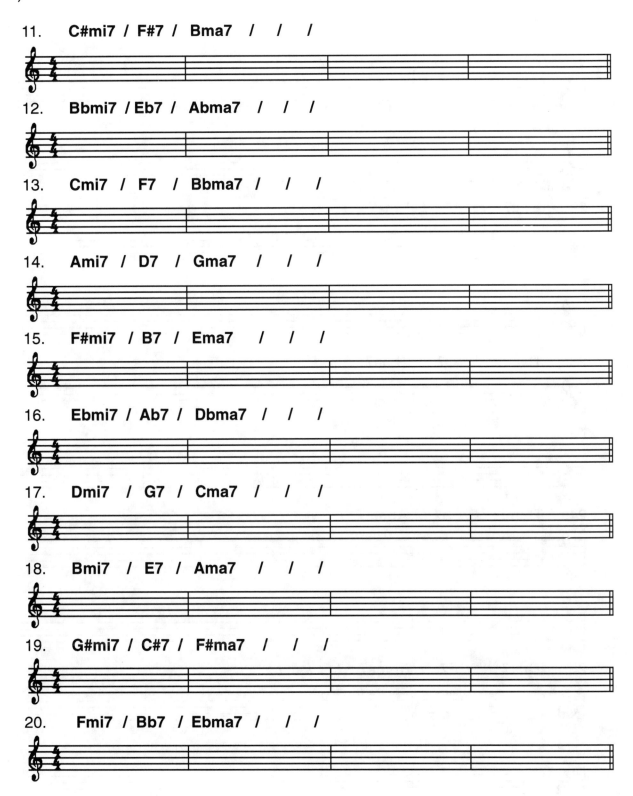

12. **Bbmi7 / Eb7 / Abma7 / / /**

13. **Cmi7 / F7 / Bbma7 / / /**

14. **Ami7 / D7 / Gma7 / / /**

15. **F#mi7 / B7 / Ema7 / / /**

16. **Ebmi7 / Ab7 / Dbma7 / / /**

17. **Dmi7 / G7 / Cma7 / / /**

18. **Bmi7 / E7 / Ama7 / / /**

19. **G#mi7 / C#7 / F#ma7 / / /**

20. **Fmi7 / Bb7 / Ebma7 / / /**

(contd)

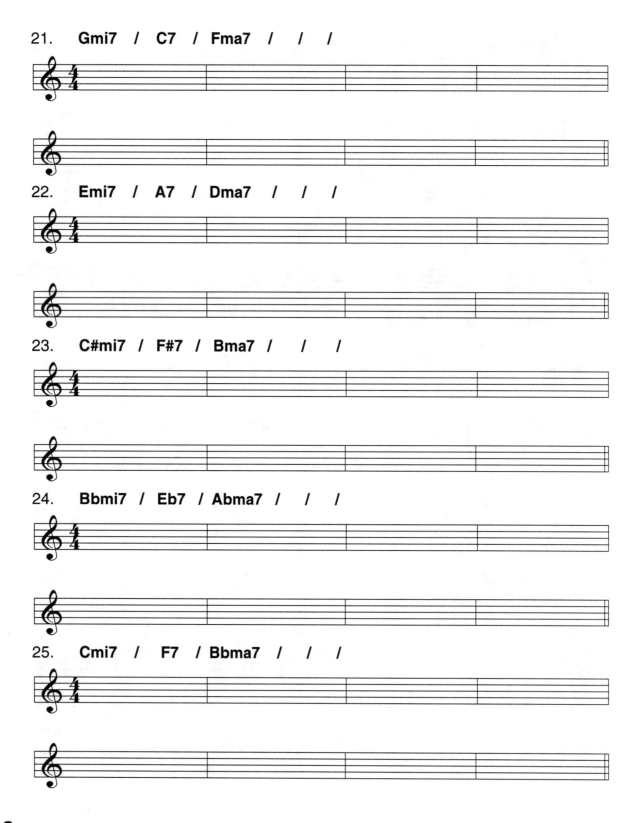

21. Gmi7 / C7 / Fma7 / / /

22. Emi7 / A7 / Dma7 / / /

23. C#mi7 / F#7 / Bma7 / / /

24. Bbmi7 / Eb7 / Abma7 / / /

25. Cmi7 / F7 / Bbma7 / / /

(contd)

26. **Ami7 / D7 / Gma7 / / /**

27. **F#mi7 / B7 / Ema7 / / /**

28. **Ebmi7 / Ab7 / Dbma7 / / /**

29. **Dmi7 / G7 / Cma7 / / /**

30. **Bmi7 / E7 / Ama7 / / /**

(contd)

31. **Dmi7 / G7 / Cma7 / / /**

32. **Dmi7 / G7 / Cma7 / / /**

33. **Dmi7 / G7 / Cma7 / / /**

34. **Dmi7 / G7 / Cma7 / / /**

35. **Dmi7 / G7 / Cma7 / / /**

36. **Fmi7 / Bb7 / Ebma7 / / /**

37. **G#mi7 / C#7 / F#ma7 / / /**

38. **Bmi7 / E7 / Ama7 / / /**

39. **Ami7 / D7 / Gma7 / / /**

40. **Cmi7 / F7 / Bbma7 / / /**

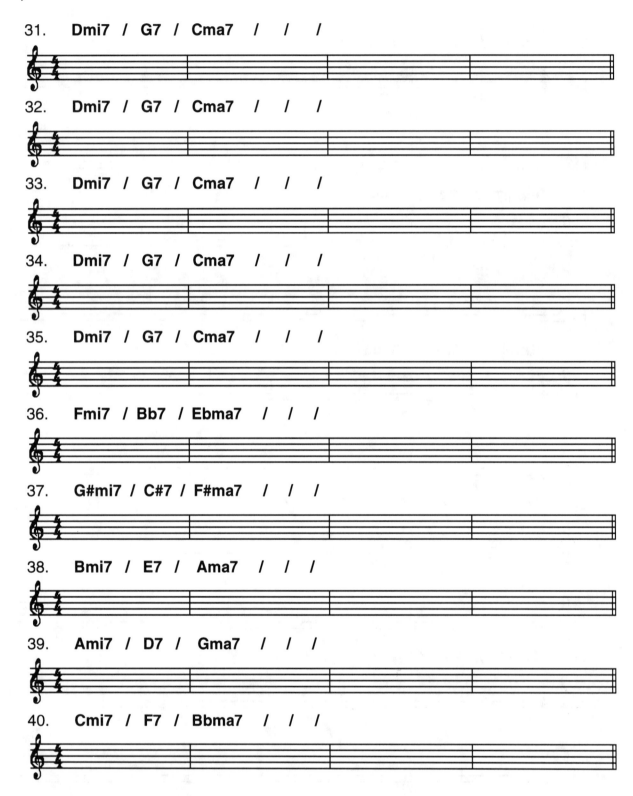

(contd)

41. **Ebmi7 / Ab7 / Dbma7 / / /**

42. **F#mi7 / B7 / Ema7 / / /**

43. **Emi7 / A7 / Dma7 / / /**

44. **Gmi7 / C7 / Fma7 / / /**

45. **Bbmi7 / Eb7 / Abma7 / / /**

46. **C#mi7 / F#7 / Bma7 / / /**

47. **Dmi7 / G7 / Cma7 / / /**

48. **Fmi7 / Bb7 / Ebma7 / / /**

49. **G#mi7 / C#7 / F#ma7 / / /**

50. **Bmi7 / E7 / Ama7 / / /**

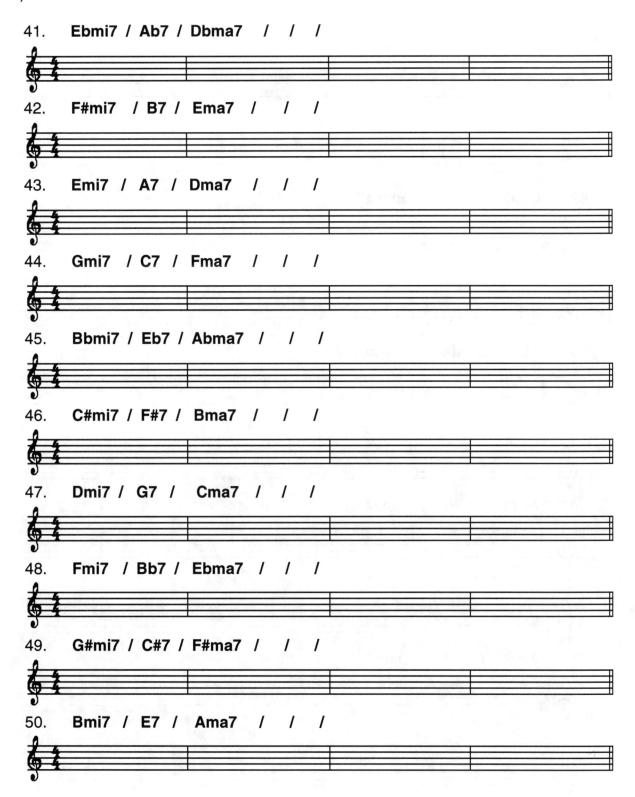

(contd)

51. **Ami7 / D7 / Gma7 / / /**

52. **Cmi7 / F7 / Bbma7 / / /**

53. **Ebmi7 / Ab7 / Dbma7 / / /**

54. **F#mi7 / B7 / Ema7 / / /**

55. **Emi7 / A7 / Dma7 / / /**

(contd)

56. **Gmi7 / C7 / Fma7 / / /**

57. **Bbmi7 / Eb7 / Abma7 / / /**

58. **C#mi7 / F#7 / Bma7 / / /**

59. **Dmi7 / G7 / Cma7 / / /**

60. **Fmi7 / Bb7 / Ebma7 / / /**

--- NOTES ---

__Note to students__ - if you are doing the Eartraining exercises, the Workbook Answers section is where you check your answers. If you are studying with an instructor, they can use this section as a source of questions to drill you on the material - otherwise you can use this section to verify your work if you are doing the exercises on a self-study basis using the cassette tapes which are available (see page __vi__).

__Note to teachers__ - if you are drilling students on this material, you can play from this Workbook Answers section, and the students can fill out their answers in the Workbook Questions section. Be sure to play __DO__ as a reference before each question in sections 4 & 5 below (diatonic triads and modes).

This part of the book contains answers for the following exercises:-

1. *Major triad progressions - 'pairs' (two chords each)*

2. *Major triad progressions - three chords each*

3. *Major triad progressions - four and eight chords each*

4. *Diatonic triad progressions*

5. *Modal scales*

6. *II-V-I progressions - pairs*

7. *II-V-I progressions - four key centers each*

8. *7-3 melodic line dictation with harmonization*

1. _MAJOR TRIAD PROGRESSIONS - PAIRS_

1.	4		26.	1/2D
2.	5		27.	1/2U
3.	4		28.	1/2U
4.	4		29.	4
5.	5		30.	5
6.	4		31.	1/2D
7.	5		32.	5
8.	5		33.	1/2U
9.	5		34.	1/2D
10.	4		35.	5
11.	5		36.	4
12.	4		37.	1/2D
13.	4		38.	1/2D
14.	5		39.	4
15.	5		40.	1/2U
16.	4		41.	1/2D
17.	5		42.	1/2U
18.	4		43.	4
19.	4		44.	5
20.	4		45.	1/2D
21.	5		46.	4
22.	4		47.	1/2U
23.	5		48.	5
24.	5		49.	1/2U
25.	4		50.	1/2D

(Voicings used on tape)

(Voicings used on tape contd)

2. *MAJOR TRIAD PROGRESSIONS - THREE CHORDS EACH*

1.	1/2D	followed by	5
2.	1/2U	followed by	4
3.	4	followed by	5
4.	1/2D	followed by	1/2U
5.	1/2D	followed by	4
6.	1/2U	followed by	5
7.	5	followed by	5
8.	4	followed by	1/2U
9.	1/2U	followed by	1/2D
10.	1/2D	followed by	5
11.	1/2U	followed by	4
12.	1/2U	followed by	5
13.	5	followed by	4
14.	4	followed by	1/2D
15.	1/2U	followed by	1/2U
16.	1/2U	followed by	5
17.	1/2D	followed by	4
18.	4	followed by	4
19.	1/2U	followed by	1/2D
20.	5	followed by	1/2U
21.	1/2U	followed by	4
22.	1/2D	followed by	5
23.	1/2U	followed by	5
24.	1/2D	followed by	4
25.	5	followed by	4

26.	1/2D	followed by	1/2U
27.	1/2U	followed by	4
28.	1/2D	followed by	5
29.	4	followed by	4
30.	5	followed by	1I2D
31.	4	followed by	1/2U
32.	4	followed by	5
33.	1/2D	followed by	4
34.	1/2U	followed by	5
35.	1/2U	followed by	4
36.	1/2D	followed by	5
37.	1/2U	followed by	1/2U
38.	4	followed by	5
39.	5	followed by	1/2D
40.	5	followed by	1/2U
41.	1/2U	followed by	5
42.	1/2D	followed by	4
43.	1/2D	followed by	5
44.	1/2U	followed by	4
45.	5	followed by	5
46.	1/2U	followed by	1/2D
47.	4	followed by	1/2D
48.	5	followed by	4
49.	1/2D	followed by	4
50.	1/2U	followed by	5

(Voicings used on tape)

(Voicings used on tape contd)

(Voicings used on tape contd)

(Voicings used on tape contd)

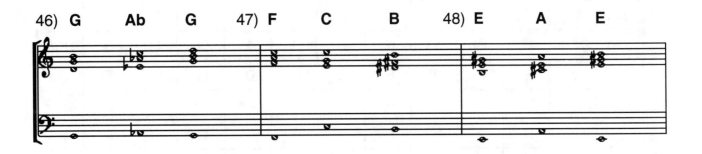

3. _MAJOR TRIAD PROGRESSIONS - FOUR and EIGHT CHORDS EACH_

1.	C	G	D	A
2.	F	Bb	Eb	Ab
3.	Bb	F	C	G
4.	Eb	Ab	Db	Gb
5.	Ab	Db	Gb	B
6.	Db	Ab	Eb	Bb
7.	F#	B	E	A
8.	B	F#	C#	Ab
9.	E	A	D	A
10.	A	E	B	E
11.	D	G	D	A
12.	G	D	G	C
13.	C	F	Bb	F
14.	F	Bb	F	C
15.	Bb	Eb	Bb	F
16.	Eb	Bb	Eb	Ab
17.	Ab	Db	D	A
18.	Db	Gb	B	Bb
19.	F#	C#	C	G
20.	B	E	A	Ab
21.	E	A	Ab	Eb
22.	A	Bb	F	C
23.	D	C#	Ab	Eb
24.	G	C	Db	Ab
25.	C	G	F#	B

26.	F	Bb	Eb	Ab	Db	F#	B	E
27.	Bb	F	C	G	D	A	E	B
28.	Eb	Bb	F	C	G	D	A	E
29.	Ab	Db	F#	B	E	A	D	G
30.	Db	Ab	Eb	Bb	F	C	G	D
31.	F#	B	E	A	D	G	C	F
32.	B	E	A	D	G	C	F	Bb
33.	E	B	F#	Db	Ab	Eb	Bb	F
34.	A	D	G	C	G	D	A	E
35.	D	A	E	A	D	G	C	F
36.	G	C	F	Bb	Eb	Ab	Db	Ab
37.	C	G	D	A	E	A	D	G
38.	F	C	F	Bb	Eb	Ab	Db	Gb
39.	Bb	F	C	G	D	A	D	G
40.	Eb	Ab	Db	F#	B	F#	Db	Ab
41.	Ab	Db	Ab	Eb	Bb	F	C	G
42.	Db	Ab	Eb	Bb	A	D	G	C
43.	F#	B	E	A	Bb	Eb	Ab	Db
44.	B	F#	Db	Ab	G	C	F	Bb
45.	E	A	Bb	F	C	G	D	A
46.	A	D	G	C	F	Bb	A	E
47.	D	G	C	Db	Ab	Eb	Bb	F
48.	G	Ab	Eb	Bb	Eb	Ab	Db	Gb
49.	C	F	Bb	Eb	E	B	F#	Db
50.	F	Bb	Eb	Bb	F	C	Db	Ab

98

(contd from previous page)

51.	Bb	A	Bb	Eb	76.	Eb	Ab	Db	C	G	D	Eb	D
52.	Eb	Ab	Db	C	77.	Ab	G	C	F	E	B	F#	G
53.	Ab	Eb	Bb	F	78.	Db	Ab	Eb	Ab	G	C	F	C
54.	Db	Ab	Db	Gb	79.	F#	B	E	F	E	B	F#	F
55.	F#	B	C	G	80.	B	C	F	Bb	A	D	G	C
56.	B	E	B	C	81.	E	F	F#	G	C	F	E	B
57.	E	F	E	A	82.	A	Bb	A	D	G	C	B	Bb
58.	A	Bb	B	Bb	83.	D	G	C	F	E	A	D	A
59.	D	G	Gb	Db	84.	G	D	Eb	Bb	F	E	A	D
60.	G	C	F	E	85.	C	F	Bb	A	D	G	Ab	Db
61.	C	G	C	Db	86.	F	C	G	C	F	E	A	D
62.	F	Bb	F	C	87.	Bb	Eb	Ab	G	D	A	E	F
63.	Bb	A	D	Eb	88.	Eb	D	Db	Gb	B	C	F	Bb
64.	Eb	Ab	G	C	89.	Ab	Eb	Ab	Db	C	G	C	F
65.	Ab	Eb	Bb	Eb	90.	Db	Ab	G	C	F	E	B	F#
66.	Db	C	B	E	91.	F#	B	C	F	E	A	D	G
67.	F#	B	F#	C#	92.	B	C	Db	C	F	Bb	A	E
68.	B	C	C#	Ab	93.	E	F	C	G	D	Eb	Bb	F
69.	E	A	Ab	Eb	94.	A	Bb	Eb	D	G	C	B	F#
70.	A	D	G	D	95.	D	G	C	G	Ab	Eb	E	B
71.	D	Eb	Bb	A	96.	G	D	A	E	F	C	Db	Ab
72.	G	C	F	Bb	97.	C	G	Ab	Db	C	B	E	A
73.	C	B	E	B	98.	F	C	G	D	A	Bb	B	C
74.	F	C	G	F#	99.	Bb	Eb	Ab	G	D	A	E	F
75.	Bb	A	D	A	100.	Eb	D	G	C	B	F#	G	C

(Voicings used on tape)

(Voicings used on tape contd)

(Voicings used on tape contd)

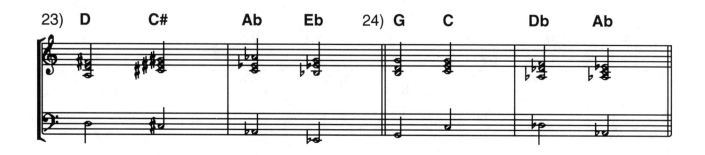

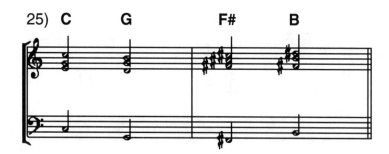

(Voicings used on tape contd)

(Voicings used on tape contd)

(Voicings used on tape contd)

(Voicings used on tape contd)

(Voicings used on tape contd)

(Voicings used on tape contd)

(Voicings used on tape contd)

(Voicings used on tape contd)

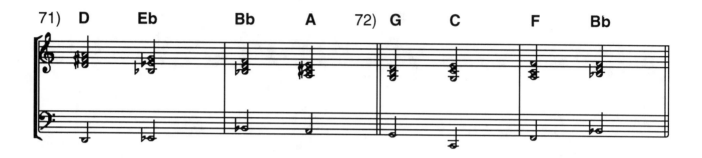

(Voicings used on tape contd)

(Voicings used on tape contd)

(Voicings used on tape contd)

(Voicings used on tape contd)

(Voicings used on tape contd)

4. DIATONIC TRIAD PROGRESSIONS

#	Key	1	2	3	4
1.	Key of C	C	G	F	C
2.	Key of C	C	Ami	Dmi	G
3.	Key of C	C	Dmi	Emi	F
4.	Key of C	C	Ami	F	Dmi
5.	Key of C	C	Bo	F	Emi
6.	Key of C	C	Dmi	G	Ami
7.	Key of C	C	F	Ami	G
8.	Key of C	C	G	Dmi	Ami
9.	Key of C	C	Bo	Ami	G
10.	Key of C	C	Emi	G	Bo
11.	Key of C	C	F	G	C
12.	Key of C	C	Ami	Emi	F
13.	Key of C	C	Emi	F	Ami
14.	Key of C	C	Bo	Dmi	F
15.	Key of C	C	F	Dmi	G
16.	Key of C	C	G	Emi	F
17.	Key of C	C	G	Ami	Bo
18.	Key of C	C	F	G	Ami
19.	Key of C	C	G	Dmi	Emi
20.	Key of C	C	Ami	F	Emi
21.	Key of C	C	G	Bo	C
22.	Key of C	C	Dmi	Ami	F
23.	Key of C	C	Dmi	F	G
24.	Key of C	C	Emi	Ami	F
25.	Key of C	C	G	C	Dmi
26.	Key of C	Dmi	G	C	F
27.	Key of C	Bo	C	F	Emi
28.	Key of C	Ami	Emi	F	C
29.	Key of C	F	Emi	Dmi	C
30.	Key of C	G	C	Dmi	Emi
31.	Key of C	G	Bo	C	Dmi
32.	Key of C	Dmi	Ami	F	C
33.	Key of C	F	Ami	Emi	G
34.	Key of C	Emi	F	Bo	C
35.	Key of C	F	G	C	Dmi
36.	Key of C	F	Emi	Dmi	G
37.	Key of C	C	Ami	Emi	Dmi
38.	Key of C	G	Ami	F	C
39.	Key of C	Ami	G	F	Bo
40.	Key of C	Bo	F	C	Dmi
41.	Key of C	C	G	Dmi	Ami
42.	Key of C	F	Ami	C	Emi
43.	Key of C	Dmi	Emi	F	G
44.	Key of C	Ami	F	C	Emi
45.	Key of C	Bo	G	Emi	C
46.	Key of C	F	Emi	C	Dmi
47.	Key of C	G	F	C	F
48.	Key of C	Dmi	Emi	Ami	G
49.	Key of C	Emi	F	G	Bo
50.	Key of C	C	Ami	Emi	Dmi

116

(contd from previous page)

51.	Key of G	G	Emi	C	D
52.	Key of D	D	C#o	Emi	A
53.	Key of A	A	E	D	C#mi
54.	Key of E	E	F#mi	G#mi	A
55.	Key of B	B	G#mi	F#	C#mi
56.	Key of F#	F#	B	C#	F#
57.	Key of Db	Db	Fmi	Ab	Co
58.	Key of Ab	Ab	Eb	Bbmi	Fmi
59.	Key of Eb	Eb	Do	Bb	Cmi
60.	Key of Bb	Bb	Eb	Cmi	F
61.	Key of F	F	C	Gmi	Dmi
62.	Key of Bb	Bb	Cmi	Dmi	F
63.	Key of Eb	Eb	Bb	Eb	Gmi
64.	Key of Ab	Ab	Go	Fmi	Eb
65.	Key of Db	Db	Gb	Bbmi	Ab
66.	Key of F#	F#	B	C#	E#o
67.	Key of B	B	D#mi	F#	E
68.	Key of E	E	A	F#mi	B
69.	Key of A	A	F#mi	D	Bmi
70.	Key of D	D	C#o	G	F#mi
71.	Key of G	G	C	Emi	Bmi
72.	Key of D	D	A	Emi	D
73.	Key of A	A	F#mi	E	G#o
74.	Key of E	E	G#mi	B	A
75.	Key of Cb	Cb	Gb	Fb	Cb

76.	Key of Gb	Db	Cb	Bbmi	Gb
77.	Key of C#	B#o	C#	E#mi	D#mi
78.	Key of Ab	Cmi	Bbmi	Eb	Ab
79.	Key of Eb	Ab	Gmi	Fmi	Eb
80.	Key of Bb	F	Bb	Eb	Gmi
81.	Key of F	C	Dmi	Eo	Bb
82.	Key of Bb	Gmi	Eb	Bb	Cmi
83.	Key of Eb	Ab	Fmi	Bb	Eb
84.	Key of Ab	Ab	Bbmi	Cmi	Fmi
85.	Key of C#	G#	F#	C#	A#mi
86.	Key of Gb	Ebmi	Fo	Gb	Bbmi
87.	Key of Cb	Fb	Cb	Dbmi	Abmi
88.	Key of E	B	C#mi	A	E
89.	Key of A	F#mi	D	Bmi	G#o
90.	Key of D	Emi	A	G	D
91.	Key of G	D	C	Ami	Emi
92.	Key of D	A	D	A	Emi
93.	Key of A	G#o	E	F#mi	D
94.	Key of E	A	C#mi	B	G#mi
95.	Key of B	B	F#	E	G#mi
96.	Key of F#	A#mi	B	C#	D#mi
97.	Key of Db	Ab	Fmi	Co	Db
98.	Key of Ab	Db	Cmi	Bbmi	Eb
99.	Key of Eb	Cmi	Do	Ab	Gmi
100.	Key of Bb	Dmi	F	Gmi	Eb

(Voicings used on tape)

(Voicings used on tape contd)

(Voicings used on tape contd)

(Voicings used on tape contd)

(Voicings used on tape contd)

(Voicings used on tape contd)

(Voicings used on tape contd)

(Voicings used on tape contd)

(Voicings used on tape contd)

(Voicings used on tape contd)

5. MODAL SCALES

	Starting note	Mode description	Relative major			Starting note	Mode description	Relative major
1.	C	Lydian	G		26.	C#	Dorian	B
2.	C	Dorian	Bb		27.	C#	Phrygian	A
3.	C	Phrygian	Ab		28.	C#	Mixolydian	F#
4.	C	Ionian	C		29.	C#	Locrian	D
5.	C	Mixolydian	F		30.	C#	Aeolian	E
6.	C	Locrian	Db		31.	C#	Mixolydian	F#
7.	C	Aeolian	Eb		32.	C#	Phrygian	A
8.	C	Mixolydian	F		33.	C#	Locrian	D
9.	C	Lydian	G		34.	C#	Dorian	B
10.	C	Phrygian	Ab		35.	C#	Aeolian	E
11.	C	Dorian	Bb		36.	C#	Dorian	B
12.	C	Ionian	C		37.	C#	Locrian	D
13.	C	Aeolian	Eb		38.	C#	Phrygian	A
14.	C	Locrian	Db		39.	C#	Mixolydian	F#
15.	C	Aeolian	Eb		40.	C#	Aeolian	E
16.	C	Phrygian	Ab		41.	C#	Dorian	B
17.	C	Lydian	G		42.	C#	Phrygian	A
18.	C	Mixolydian	F		43.	C#	Locrian	D
19.	C	Locrian	Db		44.	C#	Mixolydian	F#
20.	C	Dorian	Bb		45.	C#	Dorian	B
21.	C	Phrygian	Ab		46.	C#	Mixolydian	F#
22.	C	Locrian	Db		47.	C#	Locrian	D
23.	C	Mixolydian	F		48.	C#	Aeolian	E
24.	C	Aeolian	Eb		49.	C#	Phrygian	A
25.	C	Lydian	G		50.	C#	Dorian	B

(contd from previous page)

	Starting note	Mode description	Relative major
51.	C	Phrygian	Ab
52.	C	Dorian	Bb
53.	C#	Mixolydian	F#
54.	C	Locrian	Db
55.	C#	Aeolian	E
56.	C#	Phrygian	A
57.	C	Ionian	C
58.	C	Phrygian	Ab
59.	C#	Dorian	B
60.	C	Lydian	G
61.	C#	Locrian	D
62.	C	Locrian	Db
63.	C	Mixolydian	F
64.	C#	Aeolian	E
65.	C	Lydian	G
66.	C	Aeolian	Eb
67.	C#	Dorian	B
68.	C#	Phrygian	A
69.	C	Phrygian	Ab
70.	C#	Mixolydian	F#
71.	C	Ionian	C
72.	C	Phrygian	Ab
73.	C#	Locrian	D
74.	C#	Phrygian	A
75.	C	Lydian	G

	Starting note	Mode description	Relative major
76.	C	Aeolian	Eb
77.	C#	Dorian	B
78.	C#	Aeolian	E
79.	C	Mixolydian	F
80.	C	Phrygian	Ab
81.	C	Lydian	G
82.	C#	Locrian	D
83.	C#	Mixolydian	F#
84.	C	Locrian	Db
85.	C#	Phrygian	A
86.	C	Phrygian	Ab
87.	C	Ionian	C
88.	C#	Dorian	B
89.	C#	Aeolian	E
90.	C	Locrian	Db
91.	C	Phrygian	Ab
92.	C#	Mixolydian	F#
93.	C	Lydian	G
94.	C#	Dorian	B
95.	C	Mixolydian	F
96.	C	Aeolian	Eb
97.	C	Phrygian	Ab
98.	C#	Locrian	D
99.	C#	Phrygian	A
100.	C	Lydian	G

6. *II-V-I PROGRESSIONS - PAIRS*

1.	4		26.	RC
2.	5		27.	1/2D
3.	4		28.	4
4.	4		29.	1/2U
5.	5		30.	5
6.	4		31.	4
7.	5		32.	1/2D
8.	5		33.	1/2D
9.	4		34.	RC
10.	5		35.	1/2U
11.	5		36.	5
12.	5		37.	RC
13.	4		38.	RC
14.	5		39.	5
15.	4		40.	1/2U
16.	5		41.	1/2U
17.	4		42.	1/2D
18.	4		43.	1/2U
19.	4		44.	4
20.	5		45.	RC
21.	4		46.	5
22.	4		47.	RC
23.	5		48.	1/2U
24.	4		49.	1/2D
25.	5		50.	4

(Voicings used on tape)

(Voicings used on tape contd)

(Voicings used on tape contd)

21) C#mi7 F#7 Bma7 / G#mi7 C#7 F#ma7 / 22) Fmi7 Bb7 Ebma7 / Cmi7 F7 Bbma7 /

23) Abmi7 Db7 Gbma7 / Dbmi7 Gb7 Cbma7 / 24) Bmi7 E7 Ama7 / F#mi7 B7 Ema7 /

25) Ebmi7 Ab7 Dbma7 / Abmi7 Db7 Gbma7 / 26) Dmi7 G7 Cma7 / Cmi7 F7 Bbma7 /

27) Dmi7 G7 Cma7 / Bmi7 E7 Ama7 / 28) Dmi7 G7 Cma7 / Ami7 D7 Gma7 /

29) Dmi7 G7 Cma7 / C#mi7 F#7 Bma7 / 30) Dmi7 G7 Cma7 / Gmi7 C7 Fma7 /

(Voicings used on tape contd)

31) **Dmi7 G7 Cma7** / **Ami7 D7 Gma7** / 32) **Dmi7 G7 Cma7** / **Bmi7 E7 Ama7** /

33) **Dmi7 G7 Cma7** / **Bmi7 E7 Ama7** / 34) **Dmi7 G7 Cma7** / **Cmi7 F7 Bbma7** /

35) **Dmi7 G7 Cma7** / **C#mi7 F#7 Bma7** / 36) **Fmi7 Bb7 Ebma7** / **Bbmi7 Eb7 Abma7** /

37) **G#mi7 C#7 F#ma7** / **F#mi7 B7 Ema7** / 38) **Bmi7 E7 Ama7** / **Ami7 D7 Gma7** /

39) **Ebmi7 Ab7 Dbma7** / **Abmi7 Db7 Gbma7** / 40) **F#mi7 B7 Ema7** / **Fmi7 Bb7 Ebma7** /

(Voicings used on tape contd)

41) **Ami7   D7   Gma7** /   **Abmi7   Db7   Gbma7** / 42) **Cmi7   F7   Bbma7** /   **Ami7   D7   Gma7** /

43) **Emi7   A7   Dma7** /   **Ebmi7   Ab7   Dbma7** / 44) **Gmi7   C7   Fma7** /   **Dmi7   G7   Cma7** /

45) **Bbmi7   Eb7   Abma7** /   **Abmi7   Db7   Gbma7** / 46) **C#mi7   F#7   Bma7** /   **F#mi7   B7   Ema7** /

47) **Fmi7   Bb7   Ebma7** /   **Ebmi7   Ab7   Dbma7** / 48) **Ami7   D7   Gma7** /   **Abmi7   Db7   Gbma7** /

49) **Cmi7   F7   Bbma7** /   **Ami7   D7   Gma7** / 50) **Emi7   A7   Dma7** /   **Bmi7   E7   Ama7** /

7. *II-V-I PROGRESSIONS - FOUR KEY CENTERS EACH*

1.	C	F	Bb	Eb
2.	C	G	D	A
3.	C	F	C	G
4.	C	G	D	G
5.	C	B	Bb	A
6.	C	Bb	F	E
7.	C	A	E	D
8.	C	G	F#	B
9.	C	F	Eb	C
10.	C	B	F#	Eb
11.	C	F	Bb	G
12.	C	Bb	Ab	F
13.	C	G	D	C
14.	C	A	F#	F
15.	C	B	E	D
16.	C	F	C	B
17.	C	G	C	F
18.	C	G	E	A
19.	C	A	D	G
20.	C	B	F#	F
21.	C	F	E	B
22.	C	Bb	Eb	Db
23.	C	G	F	D
24.	C	A	D	A
25.	C	Bb	F	C

26.	F	Bb	F	E
27.	Bb	F	Eb	Db
28.	Eb	Ab	Db	C
29.	Ab	Eb	C	Bb
30.	Db	C	A	G
31.	F#	B	E	Eb
32.	B	F#	E	A
33.	E	B	Ab	Db
34.	A	G	F	Bb
35.	D	Db	Gb	F
36.	G	D	A	E
37.	C	F	D	B
38.	F	C	B	E
39.	Bb	Ab	G	E
40.	Eb	Ab	Db	C
41.	Ab	Eb	Db	Gb
42.	C#	Bb	Eb	Bb
43.	Gb	F	D	C
44.	Cb	Gb	Db	C
45.	E	A	D	A
46.	A	F#	C#	C
47.	D	C	G	D
48.	G	E	A	F#
49.	C	F	Bb	Eb
50.	F	C	G	E

(Voicings used on tape)

1) Dmi7 G7 Cma7 / Gmi7 C7 Fma7 / Cmi7 F7 Bbma7 / Fmi7 Bb7 Ebma7 /

2) Dmi7 G7 Cma7 / Ami7 D7 Gma7 / Emi7 A7 Dma7 / Bmi7 E7 Ama7 /

3) Dmi7 G7 Cma7 / Gmi7 C7 Fma7 / Dmi7 G7 Cma7 / Ami7 D7 Gma7 /

4) Dmi7 G7 Cma7 / Ami7 D7 Gma7 / Emi7 A7 Dma7 / Ami7 D7 Gma7 /

5) Dmi7 G7 Cma7 / C#mi7 F#7 Bma7 / Cmi7 F7 Bbma7 / Bmi7 E7 Ama7 /

(Voicings used on tape contd)

6) Dmi7 G7 Cma7 / Cmi7 F7 Bbma7 / Gmi7 C7 Fma7 / F#mi7 B7 Ema7 /

7) Dmi7 G7 Cma7 / Bmi7 E7 Ama7 / F#mi7 B7 Ema7 / Emi7 A7 Dma7 /

8) Dmi7 G7 Cma7 / Ami7 D7 Gma7 / G#mi7 C#7 F#ma7 / C#mi7 F#7 Bma7 /

9) Dmi7 G7 Cma7 / Gmi7 C7 Fma7 / Fmi7 Bb7 Ebma7 / Dmi7 G7 Cma7 /

10) Dmi7 G7 Cma7 / C#mi7 F#7 Bma7 / G#mi7 C#7 F#ma7 / Fmi7 Bb7 Ebma7 /

(Voicings used on tape contd)

11) Dmi7 G7 Cma7 / Gmi7 C7 Fma7 / Cmi7 F7 Bbma7 / Ami7 D7 Gma7 /

12) Dmi7 G7 Cma7 / Cmi7 F7 Bbma7 / Bbmi7 Eb7 Abma7 / Gmi7 C7 Fma7 /

13) Dmi7 G7 Cma7 / Ami7 D7 Gma7 / Emi7 A7 Dma7 / Dmi7 G7 Cma7 /

14) Dmi7 G7 Cma7 / Bmi7 E7 Ama7 / G#mi7 C#7 F#ma7 / Gmi7 C7 Fma7 /

15) Dmi7 G7 Cma7 / C#mi7 F#7 Bma7 / F#mi7 B7 Ema7 / Emi7 A7 Dma7 /

(Voicings used on tape contd)

(Voicings used on tape contd)

(Voicings used on tape contd)

(Voicings used on tape contd)

31) G#mi7 C#7 F#ma7 / C#mi7 F#7 Bma7 / F#mi7 B7 Ema7 / Fmi7 Bb7 Ebma7 /

32) C#mi7 F#7 Bma7 / G#mi7 C#7 F#ma7 / F#mi7 B7 Ema7 / Bmi7 E7 Ama7 /

33) F#mi7 B7 Ema7 / C#mi7 F#7 Bma7 / Bbmi7 Eb7 Abma7 / Ebmi7 Ab7 Dbma7 /

34) Bmi7 E7 Ama7 / Ami7 D7 Gma7 / Gmi7 C7 Fma7 / Cmi7 F7 Bbma7 /

35) Emi7 A7 Dma7 / Ebmi7 Ab7 Dbma7 / Abmi7 Db7 Gbma7 / Gmi7 C7 Fma7 /

(Voicings used on tape contd)

36) Ami7 D7 Gma7 / Emi7 A7 Dma7 / Bmi7 E7 Ama7 / F#mi7 B7 Ema7 /

37) Dmi7 G7 Cma7 / Gmi7 C7 Fma7 / Emi7 A7 Dma7 / C#mi7 F#7 Bma7 /

38) Gmi7 C7 Fma7 / Dmi7 G7 Cma7 / C#mi7 F#7 Bma7 / F#mi7 B7 Ema7 /

39) Cmi7 F7 Bbma7 / Bbmi7 Eb7 Abma7 / Ami7 D7 Gma7 / F#mi7 B7 Ema7 /

40) Fmi7 Bb7 Ebma7 / Bbmi7 Eb7 Abma7 / Ebmi7 Ab7 Dbma7 / Dmi7 G7 Cma7 /

(Voicings used on tape contd)

41) **Bbmi7 Eb7 Abma7 / Fmi7 Bb7 Ebma7 / Ebmi7 Ab7 Dbma7 / Abmi7 Db7 Gbma7 /**

42) **D#mi7 G#7 C#ma7 / Cmi7 F7 Bbma7 / Fmi7 Bb7 Ebma7 / Cmi7 F7 Bbma7 /**

43) **Abmi7 Db7 Gbma7 / Gmi7 C7 Fma7 / Emi7 A7 Dma7 / Dmi7 G7 Cma7 /**

44) **Dbmi7 Gb7 Cbma7 / Abmi7 Db7 Gbma7 / Ebmi7 Ab7 Dbma7 / Dmi7 G7 Cma7 /**

45) **F#mi7 B7 Ema7 / Bmi7 E7 Ama7 / Emi7 A7 Dma7 / Bmi7 E7 Ama7 /**

(Voicings used on tape contd)

46) Bmi7 E7 Ama7 / G#mi7 C#7 F#ma7 / D#mi7 G#7 C#ma7 / Dmi7 G7 Cma7 /

47) Emi7 A7 Dma7 / Dmi7 G7 Cma7 / Ami7 D7 Gma7 / Emi7 A7 Dma7 /

48) Ami7 D7 Gma7 / F#mi7 B7 Ema7 / Bmi7 E7 Ama7 / G#mi7 C#7 F#ma7 /

49) Dmi7 G7 Cma7 / Gmi7 C7 Fma7 / Cmi7 F7 Bbma7 / Fmi7 Bb7 Ebma7 /

50) Gmi7 C7 Fma7 / Dmi7 G7 Cma7 / Ami7 D7 Gma7 / F#mi7 B7 Ema7 /

8. *7-3 MELODIC LINE DICTATION WITH HARMONIZATION*

(contd)

(contd)

(contd)

(contd)

(contd)

(contd)

(contd)